The Ultimate Guide to

AIRBNB HOSTING

Tips and Tricks for Making Money and Getting Great Reviews.

Copyright 2023 – Martin Jerram

Introduction

Have you ever dreamed of staying in a cozy cabin in the woods, a luxurious villa by the sea, or even a castle in the countryside? If so, you're not alone. Millions of travelers around the world have discovered a new way of finding unique and affordable accommodation through Airbnb.

Airbnb is a platform that connects people who have space to share with people who are looking for a place to stay. Whether you're planning a weekend getaway, a business trip, or a long-term vacation, you can find a home away from home on Airbnb.

But how did Airbnb become such a successful and popular company? What is the secret behind its business model? And what are the challenges and opportunities it faces in the future? In this introduction, we'll explore these questions and more, as we take a closer look at how Airbnb revolutionized the hospitality industry.

The Story of Airbnb

Airbnb was founded in 2008 by three friends: Brian Chesky, Nathan Blecharczyk, and Joe Gebbia. They were living in San Francisco and struggling to pay their rent. They noticed that there was a design conference coming to town, and all the hotels were fully booked. They decided to rent out three air mattresses in their living room to some of the conference attendees and provide them with breakfast and a local guide. They called their service "Airbed and Breakfast."

They realized that they had stumbled upon a great idea: a platform that could connect travelers with locals who had extra space in their homes. They decided to turn their idea into a business, and launched a website called Airbnb.com. They invited other hosts to list their spaces, and other guests to book them.

At first, the idea was met with skepticism and resistance. Many people thought it was crazy or unsafe to stay with strangers or to let strangers stay in their homes. The founders faced many challenges, such as raising funds, attracting users, and dealing with legal issues. They had to overcome many obstacles and setbacks, but they never gave up on their vision.

They also had to innovate and improve their product, based on user feedback and market demand. They added features such as photos, reviews, ratings, verification, and insurance. They expanded their offerings to include not only rooms, but also entire homes, apartments, and unique properties. They also introduced new services, such as "Experiences" and "Adventures," which allow hosts to offer activities or tours to guests.

Today, Airbnb has grown into a global phenomenon, operating in over 220 countries and regions. It has more than 7 million listings, and more than 500 million guest arrivals. It has a valuation of over $100 billion and employs more than 6,000 people. It has also created a positive impact on the world, by empowering hosts to earn income, by enabling guests to experience authentic travel, and by supporting local communities and causes.

The Business Model of Airbnb

But how does Airbnb make money? And what are the key elements of its business model?

Let's look at some of the main aspects of how Airbnb works:

Platform for Accommodation:

> Airbnb operates as an online marketplace that connects hosts (property owners) with guests (travelers) looking for short-term lodging. Hosts can list their properties, which can range from spare rooms to entire homes, on the platform. Guests can search for accommodation based on location, dates,

and other filters. Airbnb provides a secure booking and payment system, handling transactions between guests and hosts. Guests make reservations through the platform, and payments are processed securely. Hosts receive payment after guests check in.

Diverse Property Types:

Airbnb offers a wide variety of accommodation options, including apartments, houses, villas, cabins, and even unique properties like treehouses or castles. This diverse range of options caters to different preferences and budgets. Guests can find a place that suits their needs, whether they want a cozy, private, or spacious space. Hosts can showcase their properties and attract more guests, by highlighting their features and amenities.

User-Friendly Interface:

The platform features an intuitive and user-friendly interface, allowing hosts to easily create listings with photos, descriptions, and pricing details. Guests can also browse and book accommodations with ease, using the website or the mobile app. The platform also provides tools and resources for hosts and guests, such as messaging, calendars, guides, and support.

Review System:

Both guests and hosts can leave reviews and ratings after a stay, fostering trust within the community. The review system helps users make informed decisions and contributes to the accountability of both hosts and guests. Reviews also provide feedback and recognition for hosts and help them improve their service and performance. Reviews also help guests find the best places to stay and share their experiences with others.

Host Fees and Guest Fees:

Airbnb generates revenue through service fees. Hosts are charged a percentage of the booking subtotal as a host service fee, while guests pay a guest service fee. The fees vary depending on factors like the booking amount and the type of accommodation. The fees cover the costs of running the platform, such as technology, marketing, and customer support. The fees also help Airbnb invest in new features and services, such as insurance, verification, and experiences.

Host Guarantee and Host Protection Insurance:

Airbnb offers a Host Guarantee program, providing coverage for certain types of property damage. Additionally, the Host Protection Insurance provides liability coverage to hosts. These programs are designed to protect hosts from potential risks and losses, and to give them peace of mind when hosting guests. The programs are free for hosts and are funded by Airbnb.

Experiences and Adventures:

In addition to accommodations, Airbnb expanded its offerings to include "Experiences" and "Adventures." Hosts can offer unique activities or guided tours, providing guests with a more immersive travel experience. Guests can choose from a variety of categories, such as arts, sports, nature, food, and wellness. Experiences and Adventures allow guests to discover new places, learn new skills, and meet new people. Hosts can also earn extra income, by sharing their passions and expertise with guests. Airbnb charges a service fee to hosts and guests for each booking of an experience or adventure.

Global Community:

Airbnb has built a global community of hosts and guests, fostering cultural exchange and promoting a sense of belonging. The platform enables travelers to experience destinations through the eyes of locals, contributing to a more authentic travel experience. The platform also encourages hosts and guests to interact and connect with each other, creating lasting friendships and memories. Airbnb also supports social and environmental causes, by partnering with organizations and initiatives that align with its mission and values.

Challenges and Future Directions

While Airbnb has experienced significant success, it has also faced challenges related to regulatory issues, safety concerns, and the impact on local housing markets. The company has had to deal with various laws and regulations in different countries and regions, affecting its operations and growth. The company has also had to address incidents of fraud, theft, vandalism, and violence involving hosts or guests, affecting its reputation and trust. The company has also been criticized for contributing to the shortage and affordability of housing, by reducing the supply of long-term rentals and driving up prices.

The company has been trying to adapt its business model, by complying with local laws, enhancing its safety and security measures, and engaging with stakeholders and communities. The company has also been exploring new opportunities for growth and innovation, by expanding into new markets, segments, and services. For example, the company has launched new products, such as "Airbnb Plus," "Airbnb Luxe," and "Airbnb for Work," targeting different customer segments and needs. The company has also entered new domains, such as transportation, media, and education, aiming to provide a more holistic travel experience.

In summary, Airbnb's business model disrupts traditional hospitality by leveraging the sharing economy, providing a platform that facilitates unique and personalized travel experiences for millions of users worldwide. The company has faced and overcome many challenges and continues to evolve and innovate in a dynamic and competitive environment. The company has also created a positive impact on the world, by empowering hosts, enabling guests, and supporting causes. Airbnb's story is an inspiring example of how a simple idea can transform an industry and a society.

How to Make Money from Your Home with Airbnb

Do you have a spare room, a vacation home, or a unique space that you don't use often? If so, you might be sitting on a gold mine. Airbnb is a platform that lets you rent out your space to travelers who are looking for a place to stay. You can make money from your home, while providing a memorable experience for your guests.

But how do you become an Airbnb host? And what are the benefits and challenges of hosting on Airbnb? In this chapter, we'll give you a quick overview of the potential for earning income through Airbnb, and some tips on how to get started.

1. Listing Your Space:

> The first step to becoming an Airbnb host is to list your space on the platform. You can list various types of spaces, such as spare rooms, entire homes, guesthouses, or even treehouses or castles. Airbnb has a diverse range of property types, so you can find something that suits your style and availability.

To create a listing, you need to provide some basic information about your space, such as the location, the size, the amenities, and the rules. You also need to upload some high-quality photos that showcase your space and make it appealing to guests. You can also write a description that highlights the features and benefits of your space and tells a story about yourself and your neighborhood.

2. Extra Income Stream:

One of the main reasons to host on Airbnb is to generate extra income from your property. Whether you have an unused room, a vacation home, or even a cozy backyard cabin, you can turn it into a source of extra revenue.

You can set your own price for your space, based on factors such as the demand, the season, and the competition. You can also adjust your price to match your availability and goals. For example, you can lower your price to attract more guests, or raise your price to maximize your profit.

Airbnb handles the payment process for you, so you don't have to worry about collecting money from guests. You receive your payment after the guests check in, minus a small service fee that Airbnb charges to cover the costs of running the platform.

3. Flexible Hosting Options:

Another benefit of hosting on Airbnb is that you have flexibility in terms of when and how you want to host. You can rent out your space on a short-term basis, allowing you to accommodate guests while still having the option to use the space for personal reasons when needed.

You can also choose how much interaction you want to have with your guests. You can offer them a self-check-in option or greet them personally and show them around. You can also decide how much support you want to provide them during their stay, such as giving them tips, answering their questions, or solving their issues.

You can also set your own house rules, such as the check-in and check-out times, the number of guests, the smoking policy, and the pet policy. You can also specify the expectations and requirements for your guests, such as the cleaning fee, the security deposit, and the cancellation policy.

4. Cultural Exchange:

Hosting guests from around the world also provides an opportunity for cultural exchange. Many hosts enjoy meeting people from different backgrounds, sharing local insights, and fostering a sense of community.

Hosting on Airbnb can also enrich your own travel experience, as you can learn from your guests about their cultures, lifestyles, and perspectives. You can also make new friends and connections and create lasting memories.

5. Additional Hosting Opportunities:

In addition to traditional accommodations, hosts can diversify their offerings and increase their income potential by offering other services to guests. Airbnb has expanded to include "Experiences" and "Adventures," which allow hosts to offer unique activities or guided tours to guests.

Experiences and Adventures are a great way to share your passions and expertise with guests and provide them with a more immersive and authentic travel experience. You can offer anything from cooking classes, yoga sessions, hiking trips, or art workshops. You can also set your own price, schedule, and group size for your experiences or adventures.

Airbnb charges a service fee to hosts and guests for each booking of an experience or adventure, similar to the fee for accommodations. However, the fee is lower for experiences and adventures, as they require less resources and support from Airbnb.

6. Airbnb Host Guarantee:

One of the concerns that hosts may have is the risk of property damage caused by guests. To address this issue, Airbnb offers a Host Guarantee, which provides protection for hosts in case of property damage.

The Host Guarantee covers up to $1 million in property damage for eligible items, such as furniture, appliances, and electronics. However, it does not cover items such as cash, jewelry, artwork, or pets. It also does not cover personal liability or bodily injury.

The Host Guarantee is not an insurance policy, and it has some limitations and exclusions. Therefore, hosts should also have their own insurance coverage, and review the terms and conditions of the Host Guarantee carefully.

7. Reviews and Trust Building:

Positive reviews are crucial for attracting more guests and building trust within the Airbnb community. By providing a welcoming and well-maintained space, hosts can earn positive reviews and ratings from their guests, which will boost their visibility and reputation on the platform.

Reviews also provide feedback and recognition for hosts and help them improve their service and performance. Reviews also help guests find the best places to stay and share their experiences with others.

To get positive reviews, hosts should follow some best practices, such as:

- Communicate clearly and promptly with guests, before, during, and after their stay.
- Provide accurate and honest information about the space, the amenities, and the rules.
- Ensure that the space is clean, comfortable, and safe for guests.

- Provide extra touches, such as a welcome note, a local guide, or a complimentary snack.

- Be respectful, friendly, and helpful to guests, and respect their privacy and preferences.

- Ask guests for feedback and thank them for their stay.

8. Support and Resources:

Airbnb provides hosts with various resources, guides, and support to enhance their hosting experience. This includes tips on creating appealing listings, hospitality best practices, and tools to manage reservations effectively.

Airbnb also provides customer support for hosts and guests, 24/7, in multiple languages. Hosts can contact Airbnb for any issues or questions they may have, such as payment, cancellation, or dispute resolution.

Airbnb also has a community of hosts, who can share their experiences, advice, and support with each other. Hosts can join online forums, groups, or events, where they can connect with other hosts, learn from their stories, and exchange ideas.

9. Adapting to Changes:

It's important for hosts to stay informed about any changes in Airbnb policies, local regulations, and market trends. Adapting to these changes ensures a successful and sustainable hosting experience.

Airbnb policies may change from time to time, based on user feedback, market demand, or legal requirements. Hosts should review the policies regularly and comply with them accordingly. For example, Airbnb may update its service fees, cancellation policies, or verification processes.

Local regulations may also vary depending on the location, and may affect the legality, taxation, or licensing of hosting on Airbnb. Hosts should research the laws and rules in their area and follow them accordingly. For example, some cities may require hosts to register, obtain a permit, or pay taxes for hosting on Airbnb.

Market trends may also influence the demand, pricing, and competition of hosting on Airbnb. Hosts should monitor the trends in their area and adjust their strategies accordingly. For example, some seasons may have higher or lower demand, or some events may attract more or fewer guests.

While there are numerous benefits to becoming an Airbnb host, it's essential to consider the responsibilities, such as maintaining the property, ensuring a positive guest experience, and complying with local regulations. Overall, hosting on Airbnb offers a flexible and potentially lucrative way to make the most of your space and provide travelers with unique and memorable stays.

How to Become an Airbnb Homepreneur and Rock

Hosting on Airbnb is not just a way to make some extra cash; it's a whole new lifestyle. It's a chance to unleash your inner homepreneur magic and turn your home into a thriving business. In this chapter, we'll talk about some of the benefits and opportunities that come with being an Airbnb homepreneur. Here are some of the reasons why you should give it a try:

1. Make Money Doing What You Love:

Hosting on Airbnb is not just about renting a room; it's about sharing your passion. Whether you're a foodie, a nature lover, or a culture vulture, you can offer your guests more than just a place to sleep. You can host events, teach classes, or provide services that showcase your unique skills and interests. And the best part is, you get paid for it.

2. Have the Flexibility to Choose Your Schedule:

One of the great things about hosting on Airbnb is that you're in control. You decide when and how often you want to host. You can set your own availability, prices, and house rules. You can host full-time, part-time, or occasionally. You can host during the weekdays, weekends, or holidays. You can host solo, with a partner, or with a team. It's up to you.

3. Express Your Creativity and Personality:

Hosting on Airbnb is a way to let your creativity and personality shine. You can design your space to reflect your style and taste. You can create experiences that are fun and memorable. You can craft a brand that stands out from the crowd. You can be yourself and attract guests who appreciate you for who you are.

4. Connect with People from Around the World:

Hosting on Airbnb is a way to expand your horizons and meet people from different backgrounds and cultures. You can make new friends, learn new things, and exchange stories. You can build a global network of contacts and referrals. You can be a part of a community of hosts and guests who share your values and vision.

5. Turn Your Hobby into a Business:

Hosting on Airbnb is a way to turn your hobby into a business. Whatever you're passionate about, you can turn it into a source of income. You can host a yoga session, a pottery workshop, or a wine tasting. You can share your knowledge, skills, and expertise with your guests. You can monetize your passion and make it work for you.

6. Upgrade Your Home and Lifestyle:

Hosting on Airbnb is a way to upgrade your home and lifestyle. You can use the extra income to improve your space and make it more comfortable and inviting. You can also use it to fund your own travels and adventures. You can enjoy the perks of being a host and a guest. You can live the life you've always dreamed of.

7. Make a Difference in Someone's Trip:

Hosting on Airbnb is a way to make a difference in someone's trip. You can provide a home away from home for your guests. You can offer them a warm welcome, a cozy stay, and a personal touch. You can make them feel special, appreciated, and valued. You can create moments that they will remember and cherish.

8. Learn the Skills of an Entrepreneur:

Hosting on Airbnb is a way to learn the skills of an entrepreneur. You can learn how to market your space and experiences, how to communicate with your guests, and how to manage your bookings and finances. You can learn how to solve problems, overcome challenges, and adapt to changes. You can learn how to run your own business and be your own boss.

9. Boost Your Income and Savings:

Hosting on Airbnb is a way to boost your income and savings. You can earn extra money from your spare room, your entire home, or your extra space. You can use the money to pay your bills, clear your debts, or save for your goals. You can have more financial security and freedom.

10. Grow as a Person and a Host:

Hosting on Airbnb is a way to grow as a person and a host. You can learn new things, develop new skills, and discover new opportunities. You can improve your space, your experiences, and your service. You can get feedback, reviews, and ratings from your guests. You can always strive to be better and do better.

Hosting on Airbnb is not just a side hustle; it's a lifestyle. It's a way to unleash your inner homepreneur magic and turn your home into a business. But it's not all fun and games. It also requires strategy, planning, and hard work. You need to follow the local laws, regulations, and taxes. You need to keep up with the trends, demands, and expectations of the market. You need to balance your hosting duties with your other responsibilities and commitments. It's not easy, but it's worth it. Because being an Airbnb homepreneur is an exciting and

rewarding adventure. Are you ready to join the club?
Your magic carpet awaits!

Chapter 1 ~ Understanding the Airbnb Platform

Let's look at Airbnb and how it has shaken up the hospitality industry. Airbnb is a platform that lets people share their homes with travelers who want something different from a hotel. It started in 2008 when three friends had a simple idea: renting out air mattresses to conference attendees who couldn't find a place to stay. Since then, it has grown into a global phenomenon, with millions of hosts and guests in over 220 countries and regions.

Here are some of the main features and impacts of Airbnb:

A marketplace for hosts and guests:

Airbnb connects people who have space to spare with people who need a place to stay. Hosts can list their properties, from rooms to houses, and guests can search and book them online.

A variety of unique stays:

Airbnb offers a wide range of accommodation options, from cozy apartments to vacation homes, and even quirky spaces like treehouses or castles.

This gives travelers more choices and lets them experience the destination in a more authentic way.

A way to empower hosts and local communities:

Airbnb enables hosts to earn extra income from their properties and share their local knowledge with guests. This creates economic opportunities for hosts, especially in areas where traditional hospitality is limited.

A platform for cultural exchange and personalization:

Airbnb encourages hosts and guests to interact and exchange stories, tips, and recommendations. This fosters a sense of connection and community and provides guests with a more personalized and memorable travel experience.

A source of challenges and regulatory issues:

Airbnb has faced some hurdles and criticisms, especially in urban areas, for its potential effects on housing markets, safety, and local regulations. The company has been trying to balance innovation with responsibility, and to work with various stakeholders to address these issues.

A disruptor of traditional hospitality:

> Airbnb has changed the game for the hospitality industry, forcing hotels to adapt to changing consumer preferences and expectations. The platform has also influenced hotel pricing and occupancy, creating more competition and opportunities in the market.

A builder of a global community and trust:

> Airbnb has created a global community of hosts and guests, connected by a shared passion for travel and cultural exchange. The platform uses a review and rating system to build trust and transparency, allowing users to make informed decisions based on the feedback of others.

An innovator of experiences and adventures:

> Airbnb has expanded beyond accommodations, introducing "Experiences" and "Adventures" where hosts can offer unique activities and tours. This reflects the company's vision to provide a holistic travel experience beyond just a place to stay.

To sum up, Airbnb has transformed the way people travel and stay, by emphasizing community, authenticity, and the sharing economy. However, the company also grapples with the responsibility of navigating regulatory challenges and addressing the concerns of various stakeholders in the evolving landscape of modern travel.

Benefits and Challenges of Hosting on Airbnb

If you have a spare room, a vacation home, or even a quirky space that you're not using, why not turn it into a source of income and a way to connect with travelers from around the world? That's the idea behind hosting on Airbnb, a platform that lets you share your space with guests who are looking for unique and authentic accommodations.

Hosting on Airbnb can be a rewarding and enjoyable experience, but it also comes with some challenges and responsibilities. In this chapter, we'll talk about some of the pros and cons of hosting on Airbnb, and how to make the most of your hosting journey.

Here are some of the benefits of hosting on Airbnb:

Earn extra money from your space:

> Hosting on Airbnb is a great way to generate additional income from your property. You can set your own prices, adjust them according to demand, and earn money from bookings. You can also

diversify your income by offering experiences or adventures, where you can share your skills, hobbies, or passions with your guests.

Have the flexibility to host on your terms:

One of the best things about hosting on Airbnb is that you're in control. You can decide when and how often you want to host, and set your own availability, house rules, and cancellation policies. You can host full-time, part-time, or occasionally, depending on your schedule and preferences.

Meet and connect with people from around the world:

Hosting on Airbnb is a wonderful opportunity to meet and connect with people from different backgrounds and cultures. You can share your local knowledge, tips, and recommendations with your guests, and learn from their stories and experiences. You can also build friendships and a sense of community with other hosts and guests.

Make the most of your unused or underutilized space:

Hosting on Airbnb allows you to utilize your space in a productive and creative way. Whether you have a spare bedroom, a vacation property, or even a unique space like a converted garage or attic, you can turn it into a welcoming and attractive space for guests.

Enhance your local knowledge and pride:

Hosting on Airbnb enables you to share your local knowledge and pride with your guests. You can showcase the best aspects of your community, such as restaurants, attractions, and activities, and provide a more authentic and personalized travel experience for your guests.

Network and learn from the Airbnb community:

Hosting on Airbnb gives you access to a network of hosts and guests who share your passion for travel and hospitality. You can connect with other hosts, attend Airbnb events, and participate in forums, where you can exchange ideas, tips, and feedback. You can also access resources and guides on effective hosting and keep up with the latest trends and updates on the platform.

Improve and maintain your property:

Hosting on Airbnb encourages you to improve and maintain your property to attract positive reviews and repeat bookings. You can make ongoing improvements to the aesthetics, functionality, and appeal of your space, and ensure that it meets the standards of cleanliness and safety.

Here are some of the challenges of hosting on Airbnb:

Vet and trust your guests:

Hosting on Airbnb involves opening your home to strangers, which can pose some risks and uncertainties. While Airbnb provides reviews and ratings, identity verification, and a secure messaging system, there is still a level of trust involved in hosting. You may need to screen your potential guests, communicate your expectations, and address any issues or concerns that may arise.

Protect your property and liability:

Hosting on Airbnb exposes your property to potential damage and liability. While Airbnb provides a Host Guarantee and Host Protection Insurance, these programs have limitations and exclusions, and may not cover all types of property damage or liability claims. You may need to take additional measures to protect your property, such as installing locks, alarms, or cameras, and obtaining your own insurance policy.

Manage your occupancy and seasonality:

Hosting on Airbnb can be unpredictable, as your occupancy and income can fluctuate depending on factors such as location, local events, and tourist seasons. You may need to adjust your pricing and availability to match the demand, and plan ahead for periods of high or low occupancy.

Communicate and manage expectations:

Effective communication with your guests is essential for a successful hosting experience. You may encounter challenges in communicating your house rules, amenities, or check-in procedures, leading to misunderstandings or conflicts. You may also need to manage your guests' expectations and ensure that your listing is accurate and up-to-date.

Comply with local regulations:

Hosting on Airbnb requires you to comply with local regulations governing short-term rentals. These regulations vary by jurisdiction, and may involve obtaining permits, paying taxes, or following certain rules. You may need to research and understand these regulations and ensure that your hosting activities are legal and ethical.

Invest time and effort:

Hosting on Airbnb requires time and effort, from preparing your space for guests, to responding to inquiries and requests, to maintaining communication throughout your guests' stay. The level of involvement can be demanding, especially if you have other commitments or a busy schedule.

Ensure guest satisfaction and reviews:

Hosting on Airbnb depends on positive guest reviews for continued success. You may need to ensure that your guests are satisfied with their stay and address any problems or complaints promptly and professionally. You may also need to solicit feedback and reviews from your guests and respond to them accordingly.

Hosting on Airbnb can be a rewarding and enjoyable experience, but it also comes with some challenges and responsibilities. By being aware of these issues and taking proactive steps to prevent or resolve them, you can make the most of your hosting journey. In the next chapters, we'll dive deeper into the practical aspects of hosting on Airbnb, such as creating an appealing listing, setting your prices, managing your bookings, and providing a great guest experience. Stay tuned for more tips and tricks on how to become a successful Airbnb host.

How Much Can You Really Make with Airbnb?

You might be wondering how much money you can make by hosting on Airbnb. Well, the answer is: it depends. There are many factors that affect your income potential, and you need to be realistic about what to expect. In this chapter, we'll help you figure out how to estimate your income and set realistic goals for your hosting business.

Check Out the Competition:

> The first thing you need to do is to see what other hosts are charging in your area. Look for listings that are similar to yours in terms of size, location, and amenities. This will give you an idea of the average price you can charge per night.

Add Up Your Costs:

> Next, you need to calculate how much it costs you to host on Airbnb. This includes things like cleaning

fees, utilities, maintenance, and any extras you provide for your guests. It should even include any money you have invested and/or borrowed to get your space "Airbnb ready". These costs will eat into your profits, so you need to account for them.

Think About the Seasons:

Your income will also depend on the seasons and the demand for your space. Sometimes of the year may be busier than others, and you may be able to charge more or less depending on the demand. You need to plan ahead and adjust your prices accordingly.

Guess Your Occupancy Rate:

Another factor that affects your income is how often your space is booked. You can't expect to have 100% occupancy all the time, so you need to estimate how many nights per month you can expect to have guests. This will depend on your location, your pricing, and your reviews.

Save for a Rainy Day:

> You also need to be prepared for unexpected expenses that may come up during your hosting journey. Things like repairs, emergencies, or cancellations can happen, and you need to have some money set aside for these situations.

Don't Forget the Fees:

> Airbnb also charges you a fee for each booking you get. This fee is a percentage of the total amount you change your guests, and it varies depending on the type of listing you have. You need to factor in this fee when calculating your income.

Compare Short-Term vs. Long-Term Income:

> You also need to consider whether you want to host short-term or long-term guests. Short-term guests may pay more per night, but they also require more work and turnover. Long-term guests may pay less per night, but they also provide a steady and consistent income.

Be Competitive but Fair:

> You need to set your prices in a way that is competitive but fair. You don't want to charge too much and scare away potential guests, but you also don't want to charge too little and lose money. You need to find a balance that works for you and your guests.

As you gain more experience and reviews, you may be able to increase your income over time. You can improve your listing, offer additional services, and attract more guests. You can also explore other opportunities, like hosting experiences or adventures, to diversify your income.

Lastly, you need to keep an eye on the market and adjust your income expectations accordingly. The demand for your space may change due to various factors, such as local events, travel trends, or regulations. You need to stay informed and adapt to these changes.

Hosting on Airbnb can be a great way to make money from your space, but you need to be realistic about what to expect. By following these steps, you can estimate your income and set realistic goals for your hosting business. Remember, hosting is not just about making money; it's also about providing a great experience for your guests and having fun along the way.

Chapter 2 ~ Assessing Your Property

So, you're thinking of becoming an Airbnb host. That's awesome! But before you jump into it, you need to do some homework. You need to figure out if there's enough demand for your place in your area. This will help you plan your strategy and make your listing successful.

Here are some steps you can take to check the market demand:

1. Look at Local Trends:

Find out when people visit your area the most. Is it during summer, winter, or all year round? Are there any big events or attractions that bring in tourists? Knowing when the demand is high can help you decide when to open your place and how much to charge.

2. See What Others Are Doing:

Check out other Airbnb listings near you. What kind of places are they offering? What amenities do they have? How much do they charge? This will give you an idea of what the competition is like and how you can stand out.

3. Spot a Gap in the Market:

Think about if there's something missing in the market. Is there a type of traveler that's not well served by the existing listings? Maybe you can target business travelers, families, or adventure seekers. Finding a niche can make your place more appealing.

4. Know the Rules:

Learn about the local laws and regulations that apply to short-term rentals. Some places have rules about how long you can rent your place, how much tax you need to pay, or what permits you need. Following the rules is important to avoid trouble.

5. Use Seasonal Demand to Your Advantage:

Figure out if the demand for your place changes with the seasons. If your area is popular during certain times of the year, you can adjust your price and marketing accordingly to make the most of the peak seasons.

6. Understand Your Target Guests:

Think about who you want to host. What are their needs, preferences, and expectations? How can you make your place suitable and attractive for them? Tailoring your place to your target guests can increase your bookings.

7. Offer Something Extra:

Review the amenities that other listings offer and see what you can add to make your place better. Maybe you can provide fast internet, a fully stocked kitchen, or some unique experiences that your guests will love.

8. Set a Fair Price:

Come up with a pricing strategy based on your research. Consider the market demand, the value of your place, and the costs of hosting. Setting a fair price can attract more guests while ensuring a good return on your investment.

9. Learn from Guest Reviews and Feedback:

Read the reviews that guests leave for other listings in your area. Find out what they liked and what they didn't. Use this information to improve your own hosting and create a great guest experience.

10. Think Long-Term:

> Don't just focus on short-term trends. Think about the long-term potential of hosting in your area. Are there any upcoming developments, changes in tourism, or economic factors that might affect the demand? Planning ahead can help you stay ahead of the game.

By doing your homework and checking the market demand, you'll be well prepared to start your hosting journey. This will help you shape your listing, compete in the market, and make the most of your place. Happy hosting!

How to Get Your Place Ready for Airbnb Guests

You want your guests to have a great time at your place, right? Well, that means you need to make sure your place is clean, cozy, and comfortable. Here are some tips on how to prepare your place for Airbnb guests:

1. Clean and Tidy Up:

Nothing turns off guests more than a dirty or messy place. So, make sure you give your place a good scrub, especially the bathroom and kitchen. Get rid of any clutter or personal stuff that might get in the way. Make your place look neat and inviting.

2. Make the Bed Comfy:

A comfy bed is a must for a good night's sleep. So, invest in some quality bedding, like soft sheets, fluffy pillows, and warm blankets. You might want to add some extra pillows and blankets in case your guests need them.

3. Add Some Nice Touches:

A little bit of extra care can go a long way. Think about what your guests might appreciate, like a welcome note, a local guidebook, or some snacks and toiletries. These small gestures can make your guests feel welcome and special.

4. Be Clear About the Rules and Instructions:

You don't want any misunderstandings or confusion with your guests. So, be clear about the rules and instructions for your place. For example, let them know if there are any areas that are off-limits, how to use the appliances, or where to find the amenities. This way, your guests will know what to expect and how to respect your place.

5. Stock Up the Kitchen:

If your place has a kitchen, make sure it has everything your guests might need to cook and eat. This includes pots, pans, utensils, and appliances. You might also want to provide some basic pantry items and cleaning supplies to make your guests' stay more convenient.

6. Check the Safety and Emergency Stuff:

Safety first, always. Make sure your place has smoke detectors, a first aid kit, and a fire extinguisher. Also, let your guests know how to contact you or emergency services in case of any problems. You want your guests to feel safe and secure.

7. Test the Internet and Tech Stuff:

Nowadays, most guests expect to have a reliable internet connection and some tech stuff at their disposal. So, make sure your internet is fast and stable, and provide your guests with the Wi-Fi password and instructions on how to use any smart home devices.

8. Fix Any Issues:

Don't let any issues ruin your guests' stay. Check for any leaks, broken appliances, or wear and tear. Fix them as soon as possible, or let your guests know about them and how you plan to resolve them.

9. Spruce Up the Outdoor Spaces:

If your place has outdoor spaces, like a garden, patio, or balcony, make sure they are well-maintained and inviting. You might want to add some outdoor furniture, lighting, or other amenities to enhance the overall experience.

10. Respect Your Guests' Privacy:

Your guests are here to enjoy your place, not to be bothered by you. So, respect their privacy by securing your personal items, providing window coverings, and not entering the place without their permission. Your guests will appreciate spaces where they feel comfortable and respected.

11. Keep Improving:

> The best hosts are always looking for ways to improve their hosting skills and their place. So, ask your guests for feedback, and use it to make your place even better. Whether it's updating the furnishings, improving the amenities, or addressing any issues, staying committed to improvement will help you succeed as an Airbnb host.

By following these tips, you can make sure your place is ready for Airbnb guests. A well-prepared place will not only create a welcoming environment, but also set the stage for positive reviews and repeat bookings. A well-prepared place reflects your commitment to hospitality and ensures that your guests have a delightful and memorable stay, enhancing your reputation as a host on Airbnb.

How to Deal with Legal Stuff

Being an Airbnb host is awesome, but it also comes with some legal responsibilities. You need to make sure you follow the rules and regulations in your area, so you can host with peace of mind and avoid any trouble. Don't worry, we're here to help you with this guide on how to deal with legal stuff for your Airbnb property:

1. Check Your Local Laws:

The first thing you need to do is to research and understand the local laws that apply to short-term rentals in your area. Different places have different rules, and some may not allow Airbnb hosting at all. Find out what you can and can't do and follow the law.

2. Get the Right Permits:

Some places may require you to get permits or licenses to host on Airbnb. These are official permissions that allow you to operate legally. Make sure you have all the necessary permits before you list your property on Airbnb.

3. Pay Your Taxes:

Hosting on Airbnb means you're earning income, and that means you have to pay taxes. Depending on where you live, you may have to pay local, state, and federal taxes on your Airbnb income. Talk to a tax professional to figure out how much you owe and how to report it.

4. Know Your HOA Rules:

If you live in a property that's part of a homeowner's association (HOA), you need to check the HOA rules and regulations. Some HOAs may not allow short-term rentals or may have specific restrictions. Don't break the HOA rules, or you could face fines or legal action.

5. Get the Right Insurance:

Having insurance is important to protect yourself and your property from any damage or liability. Your regular homeowner's insurance may not cover short-term rentals, so you may need to get additional coverage. Airbnb also offers a Host Guarantee and Host Protection Insurance, which provide some protection, but they have limitations.

6. Be Safe and Compliant:

Safety is a priority for both you and your guests. Make sure your property meets the safety standards and regulations in your area. This includes having smoke detectors, fire extinguishers, and emergency exits. Also, make sure your property is accessible for guests with disabilities, if required by law.

7. Don't Discriminate:

Airbnb has a strict policy against discrimination, and so does the law. You must treat all guests fairly and without prejudice, regardless of their race, religion, gender, or any other factor. Be respectful and inclusive and follow the Airbnb Community Standards.

8. Respect Your Lease and Tenant Rights:

If you're renting the property, you need to respect your lease agreement and tenant rights. Check your lease to see if you're allowed to sublet or host on Airbnb. Also, communicate with your landlord or property manager about your hosting plans, and get their permission if needed.

9. Have a Guest Agreement and House Rules:

Having a guest agreement and house rules is a good way to communicate your expectations to your guests. This is a written document that outlines the terms and conditions of your hosting, such as behavior, use of amenities, and any specific rules for your property. Having a guest agreement helps prevent misunderstandings and disputes.

10. Stay Updated and Adapt:

> The legal and regulatory environment for Airbnb hosting can change over time. You need to stay updated and adapt to any changes in the laws, regulations, or policies that affect your hosting. Keep yourself informed and adjust your hosting practices accordingly.

Dealing with legal stuff may seem daunting, but it's not that hard once you know what to do. By following these steps, you can host with confidence and enjoy the benefits of being an Airbnb host. Remember, you're not alone in this journey. Airbnb provides resources, guides, and support to help you with your legal responsibilities.

Chapter 3 ~ Create an Inviting Listing

How to Write a Great Description for Your Place

Your description is your chance to show off your place and make a good impression on potential guests. A good description not only catches their attention but also sets realistic expectations for their stay. Here are some tips on how to write a great description for your place:

1. Know who you're writing for:

   Think about who your ideal guests are and what they're looking for. Are they business travelers, families, or adventure seekers? Write your description to match their needs and preferences. Highlight features that appeal to them, like a fast internet connection, a kid-friendly space, or a unique experience.

2. Start with a catchy introduction:

   Start your description with a catchy introduction that sums up the essence of your place. Use descriptive words to paint a vivid picture of your space. Show what makes it unique, charming, and inviting. Make your guests feel excited and curious.

3. Show off your key features:

Next, show off your key features and amenities that set your place apart. Whether it's a stunning view, a well-equipped kitchen, or a close location to local attractions, emphasize what makes your place special.

4. Be honest and clear:

Honesty is the best policy when it comes to writing your description. Be clear about the size, layout, and any limitations of your place. Don't exaggerate or mislead your guests. Accurate and clear descriptions lead to positive guest experiences and reviews.

5. Add some nice photos:

Photos are worth a thousand words, so make sure you add some nice photos that showcase the beauty and functionality of your space. Use a variety of photos to give a comprehensive view, including photos of bedrooms, common areas, and any unique features.

6. Tell a story:

A story can make your description more personal and engaging. Share some history, inspiration, or anecdotes about your place. Tell your guests why you love your place and what you hope they'll enjoy about it. A story can help your guests connect with your space on a deeper level.

7. Highlight nearby attractions:

Highlight nearby attractions, amenities, and points of interest. Show your guests what the area has to offer, such as restaurants, attractions, and activities. This can enhance the overall appeal of your place and make your guests more excited about their stay.

8. Explain the sleeping arrangements:

Explain the sleeping arrangements available in your place. Specify the number of bedrooms, types of beds, and any additional sleeping options. This information is important for guests in planning their stay.

9. Include practical information:

Include practical information such as parking availability, proximity to public transportation, and any unique house rules. Providing such details helps guests plan their logistics and ensures a smooth check-in experience.

10. Use positive guest reviews:

If you have positive guest reviews, use them to your advantage. Incorporate snippets or testimonials into your description. Positive feedback from previous guests adds credibility and reassures potential guests about the quality of your place and hospitality.

11. Encourage questions:

End your description with a friendly invitation for potential guests to contact you with any questions or inquiries. Being responsive and approachable creates a positive rapport from the start.

Remember, your description is your opportunity to showcase the personality and allure of your space. By carefully crafting a compelling narrative and providing accurate information, you create a listing that not only attracts bookings but also sets the stage for a delightful and memorable guest experience.

How to Make Your Photos Shine

You know the saying: a picture is worth a thousand words. Well, when it comes to Airbnb, your photos are worth a thousand bookings. Okay, maybe not literally, but you get the idea. Your photos are the first thing potential guests see when they browse your listing, and they can make or break their decision to book your space. That's why it's super important to invest in high-quality photos that showcase your property in the best possible light. Here are some reasons why quality photos matter and some tips on how to take them:

1. You Only Get One Chance to Make a First Impression:

Let's face it: people judge books by their covers, and they judge listings by their photos. If your photos are blurry, dark, or boring, you'll lose your viewers' interest in seconds. On the other hand, if your photos are clear, bright, and appealing, you'll capture their attention and curiosity, making them want to learn more about your space.

2. You Want to Show Off Your Space's Unique Features:

Your space has something special that sets it apart from the rest, and you want to highlight that in your photos. Maybe it's the cozy fireplace, the spacious balcony, or the quirky decor. Whatever it is, make sure your photos capture it and make it stand out.

3. You Want to Build Trust and Credibility with Your Guests:

Your photos are not just a visual representation; they reflect your professionalism and reliability. When your photos are high-quality, your guests will trust that your space is well-maintained and that you care about their comfort and satisfaction.

4. You Want to Set Realistic Expectations for Your Guests:

Your photos should accurately portray your space, without any misleading or exaggerated angles or filters. You don't want to disappoint your guests when they arrive and find out that your space is not as advertised. By being honest and transparent, you'll avoid negative reviews and ensure a positive guest experience.

5. You Want to Create a Lasting Impression on Your Guests:

Your photos are not only a way to attract guests; they are also a way to make them remember you. When your guests recall their options, your photos can make your space more memorable and appealing, increasing the chances that they'll choose you over your competitors.

6. You Want to Optimize Your Visibility and Bookings:

Airbnb's algorithm favors listings with high-quality photos, making them more visible and attractive to potential guests. The more clicks and views your listing get, the more bookings you'll receive. Quality photos are essential for boosting your performance and income on the platform.

7. You Want to Tell a Visual Story About Your Space:

Your photos are not just a collection of images; they are a narrative that showcases the ambiance, style, and personality of your space. Through your photos, you can convey the mood, vibe, and feel of your space, making your guests imagine themselves enjoying a cozy and memorable stay.

8. You Want to Highlight Your Amenities and Details:

Your photos should not only show the overall look of your space, but also the amenities and details that make it comfortable and convenient. From the fluffy pillows to the coffee machine, your photos should showcase the features that your guests will appreciate and enjoy.

9. You Want to Encourage Positive Reviews from Your Guests:

Your photos can influence your guests' expectations and satisfaction. When your photos impress your guests and match their reality, they are more likely to leave positive reviews, which will boost your reputation and attract more bookings.

10. You Want to Invest in Professional Photography:

If you want to take your photos to the next level, consider hiring a professional photographer. They have the skills and equipment to capture your space in the best possible way, ensuring that your photos are stunning and flawless.

11. You Want to Update Your Photos Regularly:

> Your photos should reflect the current state of your space, so make sure to update them regularly. Whether you make changes to your space, adapt to different seasons, or follow the latest trends, your photos should always be fresh and relevant.

Quality photos are crucial for your Airbnb hosting success. They are the first and most powerful way to showcase your space, attract guests, and create a positive impression. So, grab your camera, or better yet, hire a pro, and start snapping some amazing photos that will make your space shine.

How to Price Your Place Right

One of the most important things you need to do as an Airbnb host is to price your place right. Your price affects how many guests you attract, how much money you make, and how happy your guests are. You want to find the sweet spot between being competitive and profitable. Here are some tips on how to price your place right:

1. Do Your Homework:

> The first step is to do some research on the local market. Look at other listings in your area that are similar to yours. See what they offer, where they are

located, and how much they charge. This will give you a sense of the average price and the range of prices in your area.

2. Show Off Your Unique Features:

Next, think about what makes your place unique and special. Maybe you have a gorgeous view, a spacious backyard, or a stylish decor. Whatever it is, make sure you highlight it in your photos and description, and adjust your price accordingly. Unique features add value to your listing and make it stand out.

3. Think About the Seasons:

Your price should also reflect the seasons and the demand for your place. Sometimes of the year may be busier than others, and you may be able to charge more or less depending on the demand. You can use tools like Airbnb's calendar or dynamic pricing to help you adjust your price based on the seasons.

4. Know Your Costs and Expenses:

You also need to know how much it costs you to host on Airbnb. This includes things like cleaning fees, utilities, and maintenance expenses. You need to cover these costs and make a profit, so make sure you set a base price that covers your financial obligations and ensures a sustainable hosting business.

5. Keep an Eye on the Competition:

You also need to keep an eye on the competition and stay competitive. Check the prices of similar listings in your area regularly and see how they change. You may need to adjust your price accordingly to match the market conditions and attract more guests.

6. Try Dynamic Pricing:

Dynamic pricing is a way of adjusting your price based on factors like demand, local events, and booking trends. Dynamic pricing tools can automate this process for you, making sure your price is always optimal and responsive to the market.

7. Use Airbnb's Smart Pricing Feature:

Airbnb also has a smart pricing feature that automatically adjusts your price based on market conditions and demand. This feature can be a helpful starting point, but you may also want to supplement it with your own insights and adjustments.

8. Offer Discounts for Longer Stays:

One way to encourage longer bookings is to offer discounts for extended stays. Many guests appreciate the value of a lower nightly rate for booking a week or more. This can also save you time and money on cleaning and turnover.

9. Consider Your Target Guests:

You also need to consider the preferences of your target guests when setting your price. If your place caters to families, you may want to offer family-friendly rates. If your place caters to business travelers, you may want to offer amenities like fast internet or a work desk.

10. Adjust Based on Guest Feedback:

Guest feedback is a valuable source of information for your pricing strategy. If guests consistently mention that they expected more value for the price, you may need to reassess your price and amenities to align with guest expectations.

11. Review and Update Regularly:

The Airbnb market is dynamic, and external factors like local events or economic conditions can affect the demand for your place. You need to review and update your price regularly to stay competitive and adapt to changes in the market.

12. Run Promotions and Special Offers:

You can also attract more guests and bookings by running promotions or special offers during specific periods. This could include discounted rates for last-minute bookings, seasonal promotions, or special deals for repeat guests.

Pricing your place right is a key skill for Airbnb hosting success. It can help you attract more guests, make more money, and create a positive impression. By following these tips, you can develop a strategic pricing strategy that works for you and your guests. Remember, pricing is not a one-time thing; it's an ongoing process that requires research, experimentation, and adjustment.

Chapter 4 ~ Enhancing the Guest Experience

How to Wow Your Guests with Great Service

Great service is what makes your guests happy and loyal. It's not just about providing a place to stay; it's about creating a memorable experience that makes them feel welcome and valued. Here are some tips on how to wow your guests with great service:

1. Communicate Clearly and Quickly:

> Communication is the key to a smooth and positive guest experience. Answer inquiries and messages as soon as possible and provide clear and helpful information. Let your guests know what to expect, how to check in, and any other important details.

2. Make Check-In Easy and Friendly:

> Make sure your check-in process is easy and friendly for your guests. Give them detailed instructions on how to access your property and be available to help if they have any issues. A smooth check-in sets the tone for their stay.

3. Be Responsive and Helpful:

Be responsive and helpful to your guests throughout their stay. If they have any questions, concerns, or issues, address them promptly and professionally. Whether it's fixing a leaky faucet or giving them local tips, being attentive to their needs shows that you care.

4. Add Some Personal Touches:

Add some personal touches to make your guests feel special. Consider leaving a welcome note, some local treats, or a small gift. These thoughtful gestures show your appreciation and make a great first impression.

5. Share Your Local Knowledge:

Share your local knowledge with your guests. Provide a guidebook or share your favorite local spots, restaurants, and attractions. Helping your guests make the most of their time in your area adds value to their stay.

6. Be Flexible and Accommodating:

Be flexible and accommodating when possible. Consider guest requests for early check-ins or late check-outs if it works with your schedule. Showing flexibility makes your guests feel more comfortable and satisfied.

7. Anticipate and Solve Problems:

Anticipate and solve problems before they become bigger issues. Whether it's providing extra blankets during colder seasons or offering solutions to unexpected challenges, being proactive shows your commitment to guest comfort.

8. Keep Your Place Clean and Cozy:

Keep your place clean and cozy for your guests. A well-maintained and tidy space makes a positive impression and contributes to a comfortable stay. Regularly inspect and clean your property to ensure that it meets your guests' expectations.

9. Respect Your Guests' Privacy:

Respect your guests' privacy during their stay. Let them know if there are any areas that are off-limits and make sure they feel secure in their temporary home. Balancing hospitality with respect for privacy is essential.

10. Make Check-Out Simple and Grateful:

Make check-out simple and grateful for your guests. Provide clear instructions on what to do when they leave and thank them for their stay. A positive check-out experience leaves a lasting impression on your guests.

11. Ask for and Value Feedback:

Ask for and value feedback from your guests. Use reviews as a way to learn and improve your hosting skills and your property. Guest feedback is invaluable for refining your service and enhancing your reputation.

12. Handle Negative Reviews Professionally:

If you get negative reviews, handle them professionally and constructively. Respond to the concerns and offer solutions. Showing that you care and that you're willing to resolve issues shows your dedication to guest satisfaction.

13. Stay in Touch with Your Guests:

Stay in touch with your guests even after their stay. Follow up with a thank-you message and ask them if they have any additional feedback. Staying in touch shows your appreciation and builds a lasting relationship.

Great service is what sets you apart as an Airbnb host. It's not just about providing a place to stay; it's about creating a memorable experience that makes your guests feel welcome and valued. By following these tips, you can wow your guests with great service and earn their trust, loyalty, and referrals. Remember, hosting is not just a business; it's a passion.

How to Add Some Personality to Your Space

One of the best ways to make your guests happy and loyal is to add some personality to your space. It's not just about having a nice place to stay; it's about creating a memorable experience that makes them feel welcome and special. Here are some tips on how to add some personality to your space and leave a lasting impression:

1. Write a Personal Welcome Note:

A personal welcome note is a simple but effective way to make your guests feel welcome. Write a note expressing your excitement about their stay, giving them some essential information about your space, and sharing any special details that will make their stay better. This gesture sets a positive tone from the start.

2. Leave Some Local Treats and Snacks:

A selection of local treats and snacks is a great way to introduce your guests to the local flavor. Whether it's regional specialties, fresh produce, or homemade goodies, leaving some treats for your guests to enjoy adds a delightful touch to their stay.

3. Customize Your Amenities:

Consider customizing your amenities based on your guests' preferences. If you know they like a certain type of tea or coffee, stock the kitchen accordingly. Customized amenities show that you've thoughtfully considered their needs.

4. Decorate with Art and Personality:

Decorate your space with art and personality that reflects your style or the local culture. Whether it's handmade artwork, unique sculptures, or local crafts, these elements add character and charm to your space and create a memorable ambiance.

5. Create a Local Guidebook:

Create a local guidebook with your recommendations for nearby attractions, restaurants, and activities. Include personal stories or anecdotes about your favorite spots. This guidebook becomes a valuable resource for guests seeking an authentic local experience.

6. Use Themed Decorations:

Use themed decorations that match the overall aesthetic or unique features of your space. Whether it's beach-inspired decor for a coastal property or vintage touches for a historic home, themed decorations enhance the overall atmosphere.

7. Leave Personal Notes and Messages:

Leave small, personal notes or messages throughout your space. This could include notes on the bathroom mirror, bedside table, or kitchen counter. These thoughtful messages add a personal touch and convey a sense of care.

8. Create a Cozy Reading Nook:

Create a cozy reading nook with a selection of books that cater to diverse interests. Consider adding a comfortable chair or blanket to encourage guests to unwind and enjoy a good book during their stay.

9. Showcase Local Artisans' Creations:

Showcase the work of local artisans by incorporating their creations into your space. This could be handmade ceramics, textiles, or other locally crafted items. Supporting local artists adds a unique and authentic dimension to your space.

10. Prepare a Personalized Welcome Basket:

Prepare a personalized welcome basket with items tailored to your guests' preferences. This could include a selection of teas, snacks, or even small gifts that match their interests. A welcome basket conveys thoughtfulness and consideration.

11. Update Your Decor for Different Seasons and Holidays:

Update your decor to reflect different seasons and holidays. Seasonal decorations add a touch of festivity and create a dynamic and ever-changing environment for guests returning for multiple stays.

12. Interactive Guest Book:

Provide an interactive guest book for guests to share their experiences, recommendations, and memories. Encourage them to leave notes, drawings, or mementos. An interactive guest book fosters a sense of community and connection among guests.

13. Celebrate Special Occasions with Your Guests:

If your guests are celebrating a special occasion during their stay, acknowledge it with a small celebration. This could be a bottle of champagne for an anniversary or a birthday card for guests celebrating their birthdays. Celebrating these milestones enhances the overall guest experience.

Adding personality to your space is a great way to make your guests happy and loyal. It's not just about having a nice place to stay; it's about creating a memorable experience that makes them feel welcome and special. By following these tips, you can add some personality to your space and leave a lasting impression on your guests. Remember, hosting is not just a business; it's a passion.

How to Make a Guidebook for Your Guests

A guidebook is a great way to share your knowledge and tips with your guests. It's like a manual that tells them everything they need to know about your place and the area. A good guidebook can make your guests' stay easier, more enjoyable, and more memorable. Here are some tips on how to make a guidebook for your guests:

1. Start with a Warm Welcome:

> Start your guidebook with a warm and friendly welcome. Tell them how excited you are to have them as your guests and how much you want them to have a wonderful time. A nice welcome makes them feel appreciated and sets the tone for the rest of the guidebook.

2. Give Them the Basics:

> Next, give them the basic information about your place. This should include practical details like how to check in, what the house rules are, how to use the Wi-Fi, and any other important features of your space. Giving them clear and helpful information makes their stay smooth and hassle-free.

3. Be Prepared for Emergencies:

Include a section with emergency contacts and procedures. Give them the phone numbers of local emergency services, the nearest hospital, and any other relevant contacts. Also, tell them what to do in case of an emergency within your place, like a fire or a power outage. Guest safety is a top priority.

4. Tell Them How to Get Around:

Tell them about the transportation options available in your area. Give them details about public transportation, taxi services, rideshare options, and any other ways to get around. This information helps them explore the area with ease.

5. Share Your Favorite Places to Eat and Drink:

Share your favorite places to eat and drink in your area. Tell them about the best restaurants, cafes, and bars, and what makes them special. Give them a variety of options to suit different tastes and budgets.

6. Show Them the Best Attractions and Sights:

Show them the best attractions and sights in your area. Tell them about the historical landmarks, scenic spots, or cultural attractions, and what makes them worth visiting. Give them details on opening hours, admission fees, and any insider tips.

7. Suggest Some Fun Activities and Recreation:

Suggest some fun activities and recreation in your area. If your place is known for outdoor activities, tell them about the hiking trails, parks, or water-based activities. If your place is more urban, tell them about the shopping areas, museums, or theaters.

8. Recommend Some Local Services and Amenities:

Recommend some local services and amenities that your guests might need during their stay. This includes grocery stores, pharmacies, banks, and medical facilities. Knowing where to find essential services adds convenience for your guests.

9. Make a Custom Map and Directions:

Make a custom map with highlighted points of interest and directions to important locations. Whether it's the nearest public transportation station, a recommended walking route, or the path to a popular attraction, visual aids can be very helpful.

10. Cater to Specific Interests or Niches:

Cater to specific interests or niches that your guests might have. Whether they are foodies, history buffs, or nature lovers, give them specialized recommendations that match their passions. Personalized suggestions make their stay more enjoyable.

11. Guest Feedback and Contributions:

Encourage guests to provide feedback and share their own recommendations. Create a section in the guidebook where guests can leave notes or comments about their favorite local discoveries. This interactive element fosters a sense of community among guests.

12. Regular Updates and Revisions:

Commit to regularly updating the guidebook. Local establishments may open or close, and events may change. Keeping the information current ensures that guests receive the most accurate and up-to-date recommendations.

A well-curated guidebook not only helps guests navigate the local area but also enhances their overall experience, showcasing your commitment to ensuring a memorable stay. By providing valuable insights and personal recommendations, you contribute to the sense of hospitality that defines the Airbnb hosting experience.

Chapter 5 ~ Managing Bookings and Reservations

Setting Up an Effective Booking System

A streamlined and effective booking system is essential for the success of your Airbnb hosting venture. From managing reservations to optimizing your property's occupancy, here's a comprehensive guide on setting up an efficient booking system:

1. Syncing Calendars:

> Start by syncing your Airbnb calendar with other online booking platforms you may use. This ensures that your availability is consistent across all platforms, reducing the risk of double bookings. Airbnb provides calendar syncing features for popular third-party platforms.

2. Real-Time Updates:

> Enable real-time updates for your calendar. This feature allows your Airbnb listing to reflect changes in availability immediately. Whether you receive a

booking on another platform or manually block dates, real-time updates maintain accuracy.

3. Use Airbnb's Booking Settings:

Leverage Airbnb's booking settings to customize your reservation preferences. You can choose between accepting reservations instantly or manually approving each request. Tailor these settings to align with your hosting style and preferences.

4. Set Clear Booking Policies:

Establish clear booking policies and communicate them effectively. Clearly outline your cancellation policy, house rules, and any other important details related to bookings. Transparent policies contribute to positive guest experiences and minimize misunderstandings.

5. Calendar Blocking for Maintenance:

Utilize the calendar blocking feature to mark dates for property maintenance or personal use. Blocking specific dates ensures that guests cannot book during those times. This feature is handy for keeping your property in top condition and accommodating your schedule.

6. Optimize Minimum and Maximum Stay Settings:

Customize your minimum and maximum stay settings based on your preferences. If you prefer longer-term bookings, set a minimum stay requirement. Conversely, if you're open to short-term stays, adjust your settings accordingly. Finding the right balance aligns with your hosting goals.

7. Implement Dynamic Pricing:

Consider implementing dynamic pricing strategies to optimize your rates based on factors such as demand, local events, and seasonality. Dynamic pricing tools, including those provided by Airbnb, can help you adjust rates dynamically for maximum occupancy and revenue.

8. Utilize the Airbnb Smart Pricing Feature:

Take advantage of Airbnb's Smart Pricing feature. This tool automatically adjusts your rates based on market conditions, demand, and other factors. While Smart Pricing can be a helpful starting point, supplement it with your insights to ensure competitive rates.

9. Promotions and Special Offers:

Explore promotional strategies to attract bookings during specific periods. Offer special discounts or packages for guests booking for extended stays, last-minute bookings, or during off-peak seasons. Promotions can help optimize your booking calendar.

10. Effective Communication with Guests:

Establish clear and effective communication with guests during the booking process. Respond promptly to inquiries, provide any necessary clarifications, and confirm bookings with a welcoming message. Effective communication sets a positive tone for the guest's entire stay.

11. Regularly Review and Adjust:

Regularly review your booking system performance and adjust your strategies as needed. Analyze booking patterns, guest feedback, and market trends to refine your approach. Staying adaptable ensures that your booking system remains effective over time.

12. Utilize Calendar Notes:

Take advantage of calendar notes to jot down important information related to specific dates. Whether it's a reminder for a guest check-in, a scheduled maintenance task, or a local event affecting demand, calendar notes help you stay organized and informed.

13. Adopt a Channel Manager:

If you're listing your property on multiple platforms, consider using a channel manager. Channel managers automate the synchronization of your calendars, preventing double bookings and ensuring consistent availability across all platforms.

14. Guest Screening and Verification:

Implement guest screening and verification measures. Airbnb provides tools to help verify guest identities, and you can set criteria for guest reservations. Screen guests based on your preferences to ensure a comfortable and secure hosting experience.

Setting up an effective booking system requires attention to detail, responsiveness, and a strategic approach. By optimizing your calendar, implementing dynamic pricing, and staying attuned to market trends, you create a booking system that maximizes your property's occupancy while aligning with your hosting goals.

Managing the Airbnb Calendar

Effectively managing your Airbnb calendar is a fundamental aspect of successful hosting. A well-maintained calendar not only prevents double bookings but also allows you to optimize your property's occupancy and adapt to changing market conditions. Here's a guide on how to master the art of managing your Airbnb calendar:

1. Syncing Calendars:

> Begin by syncing your Airbnb calendar with other platforms where your property is listed. This ensures that availability is consistent across all channels, reducing the risk of double bookings. Airbnb provides integration options for many third-party platforms.

2. Real-Time Updates:

Enable real-time updates for your calendar. This feature ensures that changes in availability are reflected immediately. Whether a booking is made on another platform, or you manually block dates, real-time updates maintain accuracy and prevent potential issues.

3. Use Airbnb's Booking Settings:

Familiarize yourself with Airbnb's booking settings and customize them according to your preferences. Decide whether you want to accept reservations instantly or manually approve each request. Adjusting these settings aligns with your preferred level of control over the booking process.

4. Set Clear Booking Policies:

Establish clear and transparent booking policies. Clearly communicate your cancellation policy, house rules, and any other essential details related to reservations. Transparent policies contribute to positive guest experiences and reduce the likelihood of misunderstandings.

5. Calendar Blocking for Maintenance:

Utilize the calendar blocking feature to mark dates for property maintenance or personal use. Blocking specific dates ensures that guests cannot book during those times. This feature is crucial for keeping your property in top condition and accommodating your schedule.

6. Optimize Minimum and Maximum Stay Settings:

Tailor your minimum and maximum stay settings to align with your hosting goals. If you prefer longer-term bookings, set a minimum stay requirement. Adjusting these settings allows you to attract the type of guests that align with your hosting preferences.

7. Implement Dynamic Pricing:

Consider implementing dynamic pricing strategies to optimize your rates based on demand, local events, and seasonality. Dynamic pricing tools, including those offered by Airbnb, can help you adjust rates dynamically for maximum occupancy and revenue.

8. Utilize the Airbnb Smart Pricing Feature:

Take advantage of Airbnb's Smart Pricing feature. This tool automatically adjusts your rates based on market conditions, demand, and other factors. While Smart Pricing can be a helpful starting point, supplement it with your insights to ensure competitive rates.

9. Promotions and Special Offers:

Explore promotional strategies to attract bookings during specific periods. Offer special discounts or packages for guests booking for extended stays, last-minute bookings, or during off-peak seasons. Promotions can help optimize your booking calendar.

10. Effective Communication with Guests:

Establish clear and effective communication with guests during the booking process. Respond promptly to inquiries, provide any necessary clarifications, and confirm bookings with a welcoming message. Effective communication sets a positive tone for the guest's entire stay.

11. Regularly Review and Adjust:

Regularly review your calendar performance and adjust your strategies as needed. Analyze booking patterns, guest feedback, and market trends to refine your approach. Staying adaptable ensures that your calendar management remains effective over time.

12. Utilize Calendar Notes:

Take advantage of calendar notes to jot down important information related to specific dates. Whether it's a reminder for a guest check-in, a scheduled maintenance task, or a local event affecting demand, calendar notes help you stay organized and informed.

13. Adopt a Channel Manager:

If you're listing your property on multiple platforms, consider using a channel manager. Channel managers automate the synchronization of your calendars, preventing double bookings and ensuring consistent availability across all platforms.

14. Guest Screening and Verification:

> Implement guest screening and verification measures. Airbnb provides tools to help verify guest identities, and you can set criteria for guest reservations. Screen guests based on your preferences to ensure a comfortable and secure hosting experience.

Mastering the management of your Airbnb calendar is a foundational skill for successful hosting. By optimizing availability, staying responsive to market trends, and using the features provided by Airbnb, you create a booking calendar that not only prevents logistical issues but also maximizes your property's potential for bookings and revenue.

Dealing with Cancellations and Handling Guest Inquiries

As an Airbnb host, navigating cancellations and responding to guest inquiries are integral parts of managing a successful hosting venture. Here's a comprehensive guide on how to effectively handle cancellations and respond to guest inquiries:

1. Understanding Airbnb's Cancellation Policies:

Familiarize yourself with Airbnb's cancellation policies, which include Flexible, Moderate, and Strict. Each policy has different refund and cancellation rules. Choose the policy that aligns with your hosting style and provides the level of flexibility you're comfortable with.

2. Clear and Transparent Communication:

In the event of a cancellation, communicate promptly and transparently with the guest. Clearly explain the reason for the cancellation, if applicable, and outline the refund process based on your chosen cancellation policy. Open communication fosters understanding and helps manage guest expectations.

3. Managing Guest Inquiries:

Respond promptly to guest inquiries. Whether it's a question about availability, amenities, or local recommendations, timely responses demonstrate your commitment to guest satisfaction. Aim to reply within 24 hours or sooner to provide a positive and attentive guest experience.

4. Providing Detailed Information:

When handling guest inquiries, provide detailed and accurate information. Anticipate common questions by including comprehensive details in your listing description. Clear information reduces the need for guests to inquire about basic details, streamlining the booking process.

5. Customizing Responses:

Customize your responses to guest inquiries based on their specific questions or needs. Personalizing your messages shows that you've carefully considered their inquiry and are dedicated to providing a tailored experience. It also helps establish a connection with potential guests.

6. Preventing Cancellations:

Take proactive steps to prevent cancellations. Maintain an up-to-date calendar, regularly review and update your listing details, and ensure that your property is well-prepared for guests. By minimizing the likelihood of cancellations, you enhance the overall reliability of your hosting.

7. Communicating Changes in Availability:

If you need to make changes to your availability, communicate these promptly with guests who may be affected. Whether it's blocking dates for maintenance or adjusting your minimum stay requirements, informing guests in advance helps manage expectations.

8. Handling Guest Concerns:

Address guest concerns or issues with empathy and professionalism. If a guest raises a problem during their stay, respond promptly and offer solutions. Effective problem-solving contributes to positive guest experiences and can mitigate the impact of potential negative reviews.

9. Utilizing Instant Book with Caution:

If you choose to enable Instant Book, be mindful of the potential for immediate bookings. While Instant Book can increase your property's visibility, it's crucial to set requirements that align with your preferences and hosting standards to avoid unexpected cancellations.

10. Refunding and Compensation Policies:

Establish clear refunding and compensation policies in case of cancellations or unforeseen issues. Clearly communicate these policies in your listing description and, if necessary, in direct communication with guests. Transparency builds trust and helps manage guest expectations.

11. Providing Alternatives for Canceled Bookings:

In the event of a cancellation, if possible, provide alternative accommodation options for the guest. This gesture demonstrates your commitment to guest satisfaction and can help salvage the situation by offering viable alternatives.

12. Remaining Professional and Courteous:

Regardless of the circumstances, maintain a professional and courteous demeanor in all interactions with guests. Even in challenging situations, a calm and respectful approach contributes to a positive overall experience for both you and the guest.

13. Documenting Communication:

Keep a record of all communication with guests, especially in cases of cancellations or guest concerns. Documenting conversations can be helpful in case of disputes or when addressing guest reviews. Airbnb's messaging platform provides a convenient record of interactions.

14. Seeking Support from Airbnb:

If faced with challenging situations, don't hesitate to seek support from Airbnb's customer support. They can provide guidance, mediate disputes, and help in navigating complex issues. Familiarize yourself with Airbnb's support resources for hosts.

Navigating cancellations and handling guest inquiries require a balance of clear communication, proactive measures, and a commitment to providing exceptional guest experiences. By staying responsive, transparent, and adaptable, you can effectively manage these aspects of hosting and foster positive relationships with your guests.

Chapter 6 ~ Utilizing Social Media and Online Platforms for Marketing Your Airbnb Business

In the digital age, harnessing the power of social media and online platforms is a game-changer for promoting your Airbnb listing and attracting potential guests. This chapter explores effective strategies to market your Airbnb business, leveraging the vast reach and connectivity of the online world:

1. Building a Strong Online Presence:

Establish a robust online presence by creating dedicated social media profiles and a compelling Airbnb listing. Craft a consistent brand image that reflects the unique features and personality of your property. Utilize high-quality visuals and engaging content to capture the attention of potential guests.

2. Utilizing Instagram and Facebook:

Leverage visual platforms like Instagram and Facebook to showcase your property. Create eye-catching posts, share behind-the-scenes glimpses, and utilize Instagram Stories to provide real-time updates. Engage with your audience by responding to comments and direct messages, fostering a sense of connection.

3. Showcasing Unique Features:

Highlight the unique features of your property across social media platforms. Whether it's a scenic view, stylish interior design, or special amenities, showcase what sets your space apart. Use descriptive captions to convey the experience guests can expect.

4. Engaging with Local Communities:

Connect with local communities and travel enthusiasts on social media. Join relevant groups or forums, participate in discussions, and share your expertise about the local area. Engaging with these communities can enhance your visibility and attract guests interested in your location.

5. Collaborating with Influencers:

Explore collaboration opportunities with influencers or bloggers in the travel and hospitality niche. Influencers can showcase your property to their followers, providing authentic reviews and recommendations. Choose influencers whose audience aligns with your target guests.

6. Utilizing Paid Advertising:

Consider utilizing paid advertising on social media platforms to reach a broader audience. Target specific demographics, interests, and geographical locations to maximize the impact of your ads. Experiment with different ad formats to determine what resonates best with your potential guests.

7. Leveraging Airbnb Experiences:

If you offer unique experiences along with your accommodation, leverage Airbnb Experiences to market your business. Create compelling listings for your experiences, emphasizing the immersive and authentic aspects that appeal to travelers seeking more than just a place to stay.

8. Implementing Search Engine Optimization (SEO):

Optimize your Airbnb listing for search engines to improve its visibility. Incorporate relevant keywords, write a detailed and engaging property description, and utilize Airbnb's amenities and highlights features. A well-optimized listing is more likely to appear in search results.

9. Encouraging User-Generated Content:

Encourage guests to share their experiences on social media by creating a unique hashtag for your property. User-generated content serves as authentic testimonials and expands your reach as guests share their positive experiences with their own networks.

10. Utilizing Online Reviews:

Leverage positive online reviews to boost your credibility. Encourage satisfied guests to leave reviews on both Airbnb and external review platforms. Share snippets of glowing reviews on your social media channels to build trust among potential guests.

11. Hosting Virtual Tours and Live Sessions:

Embrace technology by hosting virtual tours or live sessions on platforms like Facebook Live or Instagram Live. Walk potential guests through your property, share local insights, and engage with viewers in real-time. Virtual experiences offer a preview of the hospitality they can expect.

12. Monitoring Analytics and Adjusting Strategies:

> Regularly monitor the analytics of your social media and online marketing efforts. Track engagement, click-through rates, and conversion metrics. Use these insights to refine your strategies, focusing on channels and content that resonate most with your audience.

By strategically utilizing social media and online platforms, you can elevate your Airbnb business's visibility, connect with a broader audience, and ultimately attract more bookings. This chapter provides a roadmap for navigating the digital landscape, empowering you to market your property effectively in the ever-evolving world of online hospitality.

Implementing Effective SEO Strategies for Your Airbnb Listing

In a digital landscape where visibility is paramount, mastering search engine optimization (SEO) is a crucial skill for any Airbnb host looking to maximize their property's online presence. This chapter guides you through implementing effective SEO strategies to ensure that your listing stands out and reaches potential guests:

1. Conducting Keyword Research:

Begin by conducting thorough keyword research to identify terms potential guests are likely to use when searching for accommodations in your area. Consider location-specific keywords, unique amenities, and local attractions that make your listing distinctive.

2. Crafting a Compelling Property Title:

Your property title is a critical element for SEO. Craft a compelling title that incorporates relevant keywords and accurately reflects the unique selling points of your listing. Prioritize clarity and conciseness to make an immediate impact on potential guests.

3. Writing a Detailed and Engaging Description:

The property description is an opportunity to showcase your space and its unique features. Integrate keywords naturally into your description, emphasizing the amenities, ambiance, and local attractions that set your property apart. Use a conversational tone to engage readers.

4. Utilizing Airbnb's Amenities and Highlights:

Take advantage of Airbnb's built-in features, such as amenities and highlights, to provide additional information that aligns with guest preferences. Use these sections strategically to reinforce your property's appeal and enhance its visibility in search results.

5. Uploading High-Quality Visuals:

Visuals play a crucial role in enticing potential guests. Upload high-quality photos that showcase every aspect of your property. File names and captions can also be optimized with keywords to enhance the discoverability of your listing in image searches.

6. Setting an Accurate Location:

Ensure that your property's location is accurately set on the map. Precise location details not only assist potential guests in finding your listing but also contribute to better search rankings. Double-check and update this information regularly.

7. Encouraging Reviews and Ratings:

Positive reviews and ratings not only build trust but also influence your listing's search ranking. Encourage guests to leave reviews by providing an excellent guest experience. Respond to reviews graciously, as engagement with guests contributes to the overall positive perception of your property.

8. Utilizing Local Keywords and Attractions:

Emphasize local keywords and attractions in your listing to cater to travelers interested in your specific location. Highlight proximity to landmarks, popular neighborhoods, or unique local experiences to attract guests searching for those specific elements.

9. Crafting a Unique Selling Proposition (USP):

Clearly articulate your property's unique selling proposition. What makes it stand out? Whether it's a breathtaking view, exceptional amenities, or a distinctive theme, emphasizing your property's unique aspects contributes to higher visibility in search results.

10. Offering Special Deals and Promotions:

Create special deals and promotions to attract guests searching for discounts or unique packages. Utilize Airbnb's promotional tools and clearly communicate any limited-time offers in your listing description to capture the attention of budget-conscious travelers.

11. Regularly Updating Your Listing:

Stay proactive by regularly updating your listing. Whether it's adjusting pricing, adding new amenities, or updating your property's description, fresh content signals to search algorithms that your listing is current and relevant.

12. Monitoring Analytics and Refining Strategies:

Use Airbnb's analytics tools to monitor the performance of your listing. Track views, clicks, and booking rates to assess the effectiveness of your SEO strategies. Adjust your approach based on analytics, focusing on areas that drive the most engagement.

By incorporating these SEO strategies into your Airbnb listing, you can optimize its visibility, attract a broader audience, and increase the likelihood of securing bookings. Understanding and implementing effective SEO practices will not only enhance your property's online presence but also position you as a savvy and successful Airbnb host in a competitive marketplace.

Collaborating with Local Businesses and Tourism Boards

In the vibrant tapestry of Airbnb hosting, building strong connections with local businesses and tourism boards can significantly enhance your hosting experience and elevate the stay for your guests. This chapter explores the benefits and strategies of collaborating with the local community:

1. Forging Partnerships with Local Businesses:

> Establishing partnerships with nearby businesses is a mutually beneficial strategy. Local restaurants, cafes, and shops can provide exclusive offers or promotions for your guests, creating a personalized and immersive experience. In return, your guests enjoy added value during their stay, and local businesses gain exposure.

2. Connecting with Local Attractions:

Collaborate with nearby attractions, museums, or historical sites to offer your guests special access or discounted tickets. This not only enhances the guest experience but also promotes local culture and heritage. Highlighting these partnerships in your listing adds an extra layer of appeal for potential guests.

3. Showcasing Local Experiences:

Collaborate with local experience providers to curate unique offerings for your guests. This could include guided tours, workshops, or outdoor adventures. By integrating these experiences into your listing, you contribute to a memorable and immersive stay for your guests while supporting local entrepreneurs.

4. Participating in Community Events:

Engage with community events and festivals to integrate your property into the local fabric. Whether it's a neighborhood fair, cultural celebration, or seasonal event, participating and promoting these happenings to your guests adds a dynamic and authentic element to their stay.

5. Collaborating with Tourism Boards:

Forge connections with your local tourism board to access valuable resources and information. Tourism boards often provide promotional materials, maps, and insights into upcoming events. By aligning with their initiatives, you position your property as an advocate for local tourism.

6. Offering Local Discounts and Packages:

Negotiate exclusive discounts or packages with local businesses for your guests. This could include discounts at nearby spas, restaurants, or recreational activities. Providing a curated list of local discounts enhances the overall guest experience and fosters goodwill with the community.

7. Hosting Community Events at Your Property:

Transform your property into a community hub by hosting local events. This could be a pop-up market, art exhibition, or a cultural showcase. Involve local artisans, musicians, or chefs to contribute to the event, creating a vibrant atmosphere for both your guests and the community.

8. Supporting Sustainable Practices:

Collaborate with local businesses that prioritize sustainability. Whether it's sourcing local and organic products or supporting eco-friendly initiatives, aligning your property with sustainable practices enhances its appeal. Highlight these efforts in your listing to attract environmentally conscious travelers.

9. Cross-Promotion with Local Establishments:

Explore cross-promotional opportunities with local establishments. This could involve featuring each other in promotional materials, sharing social media posts, or even co-hosting events. Cross-promotion strengthens ties within the community and expands the reach of your property.

10. Engaging with Local Influencers:

Connect with local influencers or bloggers who can amplify your property's visibility within the community. Inviting them for a stay or collaborating on promotional content can result in increased exposure and positive word-of-mouth marketing.

11. Incorporating Local Art and Decor:

Showcase local art and decor in your property to celebrate the community's creative spirit. Partnering with local artists not only adds a distinctive touch to your space but also supports the thriving arts scene in your area. Feature these collaborations in your listing for added allure.

12. Contributing to Community Initiatives:

Actively contribute to community initiatives or charitable causes. Whether it's participating in local cleanup events or supporting social projects, your involvement fosters a positive relationship with the community and resonates with guests seeking socially responsible accommodation.

By fostering meaningful collaborations with local businesses, attractions, and tourism boards, you position your Airbnb property as an integral part of the community. These partnerships not only enrich the guest experience but also contribute to the cultural tapestry of your hosting venture, making your property a sought-after destination that goes beyond accommodation.

Chapter 7 ~ Handling Finances and Taxes

Keeping Track of Income and Expenses

Maintaining meticulous records of your Airbnb income and expenses is not only a fundamental aspect of responsible hosting but also crucial for financial planning and tax compliance. This chapter outlines practical strategies for effective financial management in your Airbnb venture:

1. Establishing a Dedicated Accounting System:

> Set up a dedicated accounting system to track your Airbnb finances. This could be a spreadsheet, accounting software, or specialized tools designed for short-term rental hosts. Having a centralized system streamlines the process of recording and analyzing your income and expenses.

2. Tracking Rental Income:

> Record all sources of rental income, including booking fees, cleaning fees, and any additional charges. Clearly document the amount received from each reservation to ensure accurate financial

reporting. Regularly reconcile these figures with your Airbnb transaction history.

3. Logging Expenses:

Keep a detailed log of all expenses related to your Airbnb property. This includes cleaning supplies, maintenance costs, utility bills, property management fees, and any other expenditures associated with hosting. Categorize expenses to facilitate easier tracking and analysis.

4. Differentiating Personal and Business Expenses:

Maintain a clear separation between personal and business expenses. Designate a dedicated bank account or credit card for your Airbnb transactions to streamline the tracking process. Clearly differentiate personal expenses from those incurred for hosting purposes.

5. Recording Depreciation for Tax Purposes:

Understand the concept of depreciation and how it applies to your Airbnb property. Depreciation is a tax deduction that accounts for the wear and tear of your property over time. Keeping track of depreciation is crucial for accurate tax reporting and maximizing deductible expenses.

6. Documenting Maintenance and Repairs:

Log all maintenance and repair activities related to your Airbnb property. From minor repairs to major renovations, maintaining a comprehensive record helps you assess the overall cost of property upkeep and facilitates more informed financial decisions.

7. Accounting for Marketing and Listing Expenses:

Include expenses related to marketing and listing your property. This could involve photography services, promotional materials, or fees associated with external platforms that enhance your property's visibility. Tracking these expenses helps evaluate the return on investment for marketing efforts.

8. Keeping Receipts and Invoices:

Retain all receipts and invoices associated with your hosting activities. These documents serve as tangible proof of your expenses and are invaluable during tax season. Consider using digital tools to organize and store receipts for easy accessibility.

9. Monitoring Utility Costs:

Track utility costs for your Airbnb property, including electricity, water, and internet. Regularly reviewing utility expenses allows you to identify potential areas for energy efficiency improvements and ensures accurate financial reporting.

10. Planning for Taxes:

Stay informed about tax obligations related to your Airbnb income. Understand local tax regulations for short-term rentals and plan for tax payments accordingly. Consulting with a tax professional can provide personalized guidance based on your specific circumstances.

11. Creating a Monthly Financial Routine:

Establish a monthly routine for reviewing your Airbnb finances. Set aside dedicated time to update your records, reconcile transactions, and assess your financial performance. Regular monitoring allows you to identify trends, make informed decisions, and maintain financial stability.

12. Utilizing Accounting Software:

Consider using accounting software tailored for short-term rental hosts. Platforms like QuickBooks or specialized tools like Hostfully can automate many aspects of financial management, making the tracking process more efficient and less time-consuming.

13. Planning for Future Investments:

Use your financial records to plan for future investments in your Airbnb property. Analyze trends in income and expenses to identify areas for improvement or expansion. A strategic approach to financial planning can contribute to the long-term success of your hosting venture.

14. Seeking Professional Advice:

If navigating the complexities of accounting and taxation feels overwhelming, seek professional advice. Consult with an accountant or tax advisor with experience in short-term rentals. Their expertise can help you optimize your financial strategies and ensure compliance with relevant regulations.

By adopting a systematic approach to tracking income and expenses, you not only ensure financial transparency but also position yourself for informed decision-making and long-term success as an Airbnb host. Accurate financial records are not just a compliance necessity but a powerful tool for maximizing profitability and achieving your hosting goals.

Understanding Tax Implications and Deductions

Navigating the tax landscape as an Airbnb host is a crucial aspect of responsible financial management. This chapter provides an insightful guide to understanding the tax implications of your hosting income and explores potential deductions that can optimize your financial position:

1. Grasping Tax Basics for Short-Term Rentals:

> Familiarize yourself with the tax regulations specific to short-term rentals in your region. Understanding the basics, such as tax rates, filing deadlines, and reporting requirements, forms the foundation for responsible tax compliance.

2. Differentiating Between Rental Income and Business Income:

Recognize the distinction between rental income and business income. In many jurisdictions, income generated from short-term rentals is considered business income, subject to different tax rules than long-term rentals. Understanding this differentiation is essential for accurate tax reporting.

3. Keeping Track of Rental Income:

Maintain detailed records of your rental income, including booking fees, cleaning fees, and any additional charges. Accurate tracking ensures that you report the entirety of your income and allows for proper assessment of taxable earnings.

4. Identifying Deductible Expenses:

Identify deductible expenses associated with your Airbnb hosting activities. Common deductions may include mortgage interest, property management fees, cleaning costs, utility bills, property taxes, and depreciation. Keep thorough records of these expenses to maximize potential deductions.

5. Depreciation as a Deductible Expense:

Understand the concept of depreciation and its role in tax deductions. Depreciation allows you to deduct the cost of your property over time due to wear and tear. Consult with a tax professional to determine the applicable depreciation method for your specific circumstances.

6. Home Office Deductions:

Explore the possibility of claiming home office deductions if you use a portion of your home exclusively for Airbnb hosting activities. This could include a percentage of rent or mortgage interest, utilities, and maintenance costs associated with the designated space.

7. Documenting Maintenance and Repairs:

Keep comprehensive records of maintenance and repair expenses. These costs are typically deductible and contribute to the overall assessment of your property's profitability. Detailed documentation also serves as evidence in case of an audit.

8. Marketing and Listing Expenses:

Deduct expenses related to marketing and listing your property. This includes photography services, promotional materials, and fees associated with external platforms that enhance your property's visibility. Properly documenting these expenses strengthens your case during tax season.

9. Maximizing Travel-Related Deductions:

Capitalize on travel-related deductions if you incur expenses when managing your Airbnb property. This could include travel to and from your property for maintenance or guest interactions. Keep records of mileage, transportation costs, and any accommodations during these trips.

10. Staying Informed About Local Regulations:

Stay informed about local tax regulations and any changes that may impact your hosting income. Tax laws can vary widely, so regular updates and compliance with regional requirements are essential for responsible financial management.

11. Seeking Professional Guidance:

Engage the services of a tax professional with experience in short-term rentals. Their expertise can help you navigate complex tax codes, optimize deductions, and ensure accurate and compliant tax reporting. A professional can also provide guidance on maximizing your tax efficiency.

12. Planning for Estimated Taxes:

Plan for estimated tax payments throughout the year to avoid surprises during tax season. Calculate your anticipated tax liability based on your hosting income and make quarterly payments to stay on top of your financial responsibilities.

13. Utilizing Technology for Tax Documentation:

Leverage technology to streamline tax documentation. Digital tools and accounting software can simplify the tracking of income and expenses, ensuring that you have organized and accessible records for tax reporting.

14. Keeping Abreast of Changes in Tax Laws:

Stay vigilant about changes in tax laws and regulations. Tax codes are subject to updates, and staying informed allows you to proactively adjust your financial strategies to align with the latest requirements.

Understanding the tax implications of your Airbnb hosting income is a vital component of responsible hosting. By staying informed, keeping meticulous records, and seeking professional guidance when needed, you can optimize your tax position, maximize deductions, and ensure compliance with regulatory requirements. Responsible financial management not only benefits your bottom line but also contributes to the overall success and sustainability of your Airbnb venture.

Setting Aside Funds for Maintenance and Improvements

As an Airbnb host, proactive financial planning is key to sustaining the long-term success of your hosting venture. This chapter explores the importance of setting aside funds specifically designated for property maintenance and improvements:

1. Understanding the Need for Reserves:

> Acknowledge the inevitability of wear and tear on your Airbnb property. Setting aside funds for maintenance and improvements establishes a financial cushion to address unforeseen issues and ensure the ongoing quality of your hosting space.

2. Calculating Maintenance Reserves:

> Develop a realistic estimate for maintenance reserves based on the size and condition of your property. A common guideline is to allocate 1-3% of your

property's value annually to maintenance. This provides a benchmark for creating a sustainable financial plan.

3. Differentiating Maintenance and Improvement Funds:

Distinguish between funds earmarked for routine maintenance and those allocated for improvements. Maintenance funds cover day-to-day wear and tear, while improvement funds cater to upgrades and enhancements that enhance the overall guest experience.

4. Prioritizing Essential Repairs:

Prioritize essential repairs that impact the safety and functionality of your property. Addressing critical issues promptly not only ensures the well-being of your guests but also prevents minor problems from escalating into costly repairs.

5. Creating a Maintenance Calendar:

Establish a maintenance calendar to schedule routine checks and tasks. Regular inspections of appliances, plumbing, and structural elements allow you to identify potential issues early on and allocate funds accordingly. Prevention is often more cost-effective than reactive repairs.

6. Budgeting for Seasonal Considerations:

Factor in seasonal considerations when setting aside maintenance funds. For example, heating and cooling systems may require more attention during extreme weather conditions. Tailor your budget to account for specific needs that vary throughout the year.

7. Anticipating Future Improvements:

Anticipate future improvements that enhance the overall appeal and functionality of your property. This could include upgrading furnishings, investing in smart home technology, or enhancing outdoor spaces. Allocating funds for planned improvements ensures a continual elevation of your hosting space.

8. Identifying High-Impact Improvements:

Identify high-impact improvements that can positively influence guest satisfaction and booking rates. This might involve investing in a more comfortable mattress, upgrading kitchen appliances, or enhancing the aesthetics of key areas. Strategic improvements contribute to the long-term success of your Airbnb.

9. Utilizing a Reserve Fund for Emergencies:

Maintain a reserve fund specifically designated for emergencies. This fund serves as a safety net for unexpected expenses, such as major appliance failures or structural issues. Having a financial cushion ensures that you can address urgent matters promptly without compromising guest experiences.

10. Consulting with Professionals:

Seek advice from professionals such as property managers, inspectors, or contractors when estimating maintenance and improvement costs. Their expertise can provide valuable insights into potential challenges and help you create a more accurate and comprehensive budget.

11. Monitoring Market Trends:

Stay informed about market trends and guest expectations to guide your improvement decisions. Regularly reassessing your property's features and amenities allows you to align with evolving guest preferences and maintain a competitive edge in the Airbnb marketplace.

12. Implementing Green and Energy-Efficient Upgrades:

Consider implementing green and energy-efficient upgrades as part of your improvement plan. While these upgrades may involve an initial investment, they often result in long-term cost savings and contribute to the sustainability of your hosting venture.

13. Reviewing and Adjusting Budgets:

Periodically review and adjust your maintenance and improvement budgets based on evolving needs and market dynamics. Flexibility in your financial planning ensures that you can adapt to changing circumstances and seize opportunities for strategic enhancements.

14. Communicating with Guests about Upgrades:

Keep guests informed about planned improvements or renovations. Open communication demonstrates your commitment to maintaining a high standard of quality and can even turn the renovation process into a positive guest experience.

By proactively setting aside funds for maintenance and improvements, you not only safeguard the longevity of your property but also position yourself as a responsible and forward-thinking Airbnb host. This financial foresight not only enhances the overall guest experience but also contributes to the sustained success of your hosting venture in an ever-evolving hospitality landscape.

Chapter 8 ~ Challenging and Difficult Guests

Dealing with Difficult Guests

Navigating the diverse landscape of guest interactions is an integral aspect of being an Airbnb host. While most guests are a delight to host, encountering challenging situations is inevitable. This chapter provides insights and strategies for effectively handling difficult guests and ensuring a positive hosting experience:

1. Maintaining a Calm and Professional Demeanor:

> When faced with challenging situations, maintain a calm and professional demeanor. Approach each interaction with a positive mindset, and strive to address concerns or conflicts in a composed manner. This sets the tone for a constructive resolution.

2. Active Listening and Empathy:

> Practice active listening to understand the guest's concerns thoroughly. Demonstrate empathy by acknowledging their perspective, even if you may not agree. Empathetic communication establishes a

connection and increases the likelihood of finding a mutually satisfactory resolution.

3. Prompt and Open Communication:

Respond promptly to guest concerns or complaints. Open communication helps prevent misunderstandings from escalating and allows you to address issues before they impact the overall guest experience. Be transparent about timelines for resolution and keep the guest informed.

4. Setting Clear Expectations from the Start:

Minimize the likelihood of misunderstandings by setting clear expectations from the beginning. Provide detailed information about house rules, check-in procedures, and any specific policies unique to your property. Clear expectations contribute to a smoother guest experience.

5. Establishing a Comprehensive House Manual:

Create a comprehensive house manual that outlines all essential information, from Wi-Fi codes to emergency contact numbers. A well-documented manual serves as a reference for guests and can help prevent issues related to misunderstandings or misinformation.

6. Responding to Negative Reviews:

If faced with a negative review, respond diplomatically and constructively. Address specific concerns raised by the guest and share any corrective measures you've implemented. Prospective guests appreciate hosts who are proactive in addressing feedback.

7. Dealing with Noise Complaints:

Noise complaints are a common challenge. Proactively address potential noise issues by outlining house rules related to quiet hours in your listing. If a complaint arises, investigate promptly and remind guests of the agreed-upon rules.

8. Handling Damage or Rule Violations:

If guests violate house rules or cause damage, address the issue firmly but diplomatically. Clearly communicate the consequences of their actions, such as potential additional charges. Providing photographic evidence can help resolve disputes more effectively.

9. Implementing a Guest Agreement:

Consider implementing a guest agreement that outlines expectations and consequences for rule violations. While not a foolproof solution, a well-crafted agreement can provide clarity and support your position in case of disputes.

10. Involving Airbnb Support when Necessary:

If a situation escalates and you find it challenging to reach a resolution with the guest, involve Airbnb Support. Provide a detailed account of the situation, including any relevant communications and evidence. Airbnb Support can mediate and provide guidance.

11. Documenting Interactions:

Keep thorough records of all interactions with difficult guests. Documenting communication, issues, and resolutions helps you maintain a clear timeline and provides evidence in case of disputes or claims.

12. Knowing When to Seek Legal Advice:

In extreme cases, when faced with legal complexities or persistent issues, consider seeking legal advice. An attorney experienced in hospitality law can provide guidance on how to protect your interests and navigate challenging situations.

13. Learning from Challenging Experiences:

View challenging guest interactions as opportunities for growth and improvement. Assess each situation objectively, identify areas for enhancement in your hosting approach, and implement changes to mitigate similar issues in the future.

14. Prioritizing Your Well-Being:

Hosting can be emotionally taxing, especially when dealing with difficult guests. Prioritize your well-being and mental health. Establish boundaries, take breaks when needed, and recognize when it's necessary to step back and regroup.

Effectively managing difficult guest situations requires a combination of communication skills, empathy, and a proactive approach to conflict resolution. By adopting these strategies, you empower yourself to handle challenges with resilience, maintain positive guest relationships, and continue providing exceptional hosting experiences.

Developing Problem-Solving Skills

Being an Airbnb host often involves navigating a variety of challenges and unexpected situations. Developing strong problem-solving skills is not just a valuable asset; it's a crucial aspect of maintaining a successful hosting venture. This chapter explores strategies for honing your problem-solving skills to effectively address issues and enhance the overall guest experience:

1. Embracing a Proactive Mindset:

> Cultivate a proactive mindset that anticipates potential challenges. By identifying and addressing issues before they escalate, you create a smoother hosting experience for both you and your guests. Proactivity is the foundation of effective problem-solving.

2. Continuous Learning and Adaptability:

> Stay committed to continuous learning and adaptability. The hospitality landscape evolves, and being open to new information and strategies enhances your ability to navigate diverse challenges.

Seek out resources, attend workshops, and engage with the Airbnb host community to stay informed.

3. Analyzing Root Causes:

When confronted with a problem, take the time to analyze its root causes. Understanding the underlying issues allows you to implement solutions that address the core problem rather than just its symptoms. This analytical approach contributes to long-term problem resolution.

4. Effective Communication Skills:

Sharpen your communication skills to convey information clearly and diplomatically. Effective communication is a powerful tool in resolving conflicts and preventing misunderstandings. Strive to be concise, empathetic, and solution-oriented in your interactions.

5. Collaborating with Guests:

Foster collaboration with your guests when addressing challenges. Solicit their input, listen to their concerns, and involve them in finding mutually agreeable solutions. Collaborative problem-solving creates a positive guest experience and builds rapport.

6. Building a Resource Network:

Develop a network of resources, including local service providers, fellow hosts, and professionals who can offer guidance. Knowing where to turn for support when challenges arise enhances your problem-solving capabilities and expedites the resolution process.

7. Prioritizing and Time Management:

Prioritize issues based on their impact and urgency. Effective problem-solving involves managing your time efficiently and addressing high-priority issues promptly. A well-managed schedule allows you to tackle challenges systematically without feeling overwhelmed.

8. Seeking Feedback and Iterating:

Encourage guest feedback and use it as a valuable tool for improvement. Act on constructive criticism, iterate on your hosting processes, and implement changes based on guest suggestions. This iterative approach contributes to continuous refinement and problem prevention.

9. Developing a Systematic Approach:

Establish a systematic approach to problem-solving that includes clear steps and protocols. Having a structured process streamlines your response to issues, ensures consistency, and reduces the likelihood of overlooking crucial aspects in the heat of the moment.

10. Practicing Stress Management Techniques:

Enhance your ability to think clearly and make sound decisions by practicing stress management techniques. Whether it's mindfulness, deep breathing exercises, or physical activity, incorporating stress-relief practices into your routine contributes to effective problem-solving.

11. Learning from Past Experiences:

Reflect on past challenges and learn from your experiences. Analyze how you approached and resolved previous issues and identify areas for improvement. The ability to extract lessons from the past contributes to your growth as a skilled problem-solver.

12. Implementing Preventive Measures:

Where possible, implement preventive measures to mitigate potential challenges. This could involve enhancing security measures, providing clear instructions, or incorporating guest education elements into your listing. Prevention is a proactive approach to problem-solving.

13. Seeking Guidance from Experienced Hosts:

Tap into the wealth of knowledge within the Airbnb host community. Seek guidance from experienced hosts who have likely encountered and overcome similar challenges. Learning from their insights and experiences enriches your problem-solving toolkit.

14. Balancing Flexibility and Firmness:

Strike a balance between flexibility and firmness when addressing challenges. While being adaptable is essential, maintaining clear boundaries and enforcing house rules with a level of firmness ensures a harmonious hosting environment.

By actively developing and refining your problem-solving skills, you not only enhance your ability to navigate challenges but also elevate the overall quality of your Airbnb hosting venture. Embracing a proactive, collaborative, and systematic approach positions you as a capable and resilient host who can effectively address any situation that arises.

Establishing Clear House Rules

Clear and concise house rules are the cornerstone of a successful Airbnb hosting experience. Establishing expectations from the outset not only fosters a positive guest experience but also helps prevent misunderstandings and conflicts. In this chapter, we delve into the essential elements of crafting and communicating effective house rules:

1. Identify Key Priorities:

> Begin by identifying the key priorities for your property. What aspects are crucial to maintaining a safe, comfortable, and enjoyable environment for both you and your guests? Prioritize these elements as the foundation for your house rules.

2. Clarity is Key:

> Craft rules with clarity and simplicity. Avoid ambiguity by using straightforward language that

leaves no room for misinterpretation. Guests should easily understand what is expected of them during their stay.

3. Communicate House Rules Early:

Ensure that guests are aware of your house rules well before their arrival. Include them in your listing description and, if necessary, provide a more detailed version in a welcome guide. This early communication sets the tone for a respectful and cooperative relationship.

4. Focus on Safety and Security:

Prioritize rules related to safety and security. Clearly outline procedures for emergency situations, the location of safety equipment, and any other precautions guests need to be aware of. Safety rules contribute to a secure and worry-free environment.

5. Be Specific About Quiet Hours:

If applicable, establish specific quiet hours to ensure a peaceful atmosphere for both guests and neighbors. Clearly communicate the designated hours during which noise should be minimized to respect the comfort of everyone in the vicinity.

6. Outline Check-in and Check-out Procedures:

Detail the check-in and check-out procedures to streamline the arrival and departure process. Include information on key exchange, access codes, and any specific steps guests need to follow. Clarity in these procedures contributes to a smooth and positive guest experience.

7. Address Smoking and Pet Policies:

Clearly state your property's stance on smoking and whether pets are allowed. If smoking is prohibited or restricted to specific areas, make this explicit. Similarly, outline any guidelines for guests traveling with pets, including additional fees or specific rules for pet-friendly spaces.

8. Provide Guidelines for Amenities Usage:

Set guidelines for the usage of amenities such as the kitchen, laundry facilities, and outdoor spaces. This includes rules about appliance use, cleaning up after use, and respecting shared spaces. Clear guidelines contribute to a harmonious coexistence among guests.

9. Establish Occupancy Limits:

Clearly define the maximum occupancy limits for your property. This ensures that guests are aware of the intended capacity and helps prevent overcrowding, which could lead to discomfort and potential rule violations.

10. Specify Parking Arrangements:

If your property has specific parking arrangements or restrictions, clearly communicate these rules. Provide information about designated parking spaces, permit requirements, or any alternative parking options available to guests.

11. Set Expectations for Property Care:

Outline expectations for the care and cleanliness of your property. This includes rules about garbage disposal, dishwashing, and general tidiness. Clear guidelines contribute to maintaining the overall condition of your space.

12. Include Consequences for Rule Violations:

Clearly communicate the consequences of rule violations. This may include fees for breaking specific rules or, in severe cases, the possibility of eviction. Establishing consequences helps enforce compliance and ensures a respectful guest-host relationship.

13. Be Open to Guest Questions:

Encourage guests to ask questions about your house rules. Being open to clarifications and providing additional information when needed fosters a sense of transparency and helps guests feel more comfortable during their stay.

14. Regularly Review and Update Rules:

Periodically review your house rules to ensure they remain relevant and aligned with your hosting priorities. If you make updates, communicate these changes to guests and provide them with the latest version of your house rules.

Crafting and communicating clear house rules is an essential aspect of being a responsible Airbnb host. By setting expectations early, you contribute to a positive guest experience and create a foundation for a respectful and enjoyable hosting relationship.

Handling Guest Reviews and Feedback

Guest reviews and feedback play a pivotal role in shaping your reputation as an Airbnb host. Managing them effectively is not just about receiving positive acclaim; it's also an opportunity for continuous improvement. In this chapter, we explore strategies for navigating the world of guest reviews and feedback:

1. Embrace Constructive Criticism:

> Approach feedback, especially constructive criticism, with an open mind. Embracing areas for improvement is a powerful tool for enhancing your hosting skills and ensuring a better experience for future guests.

2. Respond Promptly and Professionally:

> Respond promptly to guest reviews, both positive and negative. Express gratitude for positive feedback and address any concerns raised in negative reviews. A timely and professional response showcases your commitment to guest satisfaction.

3. Personalize Your Responses:

Personalize your responses to guest reviews. Mention specific details from their stay to show that you've taken the time to consider their feedback individually. This personal touch enhances the guest-host relationship.

4. Implement Changes Based on Feedback:

Act on feedback by implementing positive changes whenever possible. If guests suggest improvements or highlight specific issues, take proactive steps to address them. This demonstrates your dedication to providing an exceptional guest experience.

5. Encourage Private Communication:

Encourage guests to communicate any concerns privately during their stay. Addressing issues in real-time allows you to rectify situations before they impact the overall guest experience and may prevent negative reviews.

6. Showcase Positive Feedback:

Showcase positive feedback on your listing and promotional materials. Highlighting positive reviews builds trust with potential guests and reinforces your property's appeal. Consider featuring guest quotes or testimonials prominently in your listing.

7. Set Realistic Expectations:

Set realistic expectations in your listing to manage guest expectations. Be transparent about the unique aspects of your property and any limitations. Clear communication helps prevent disappointment and negative reviews resulting from unmet expectations.

8. Monitor and Respond to Private Feedback:

Pay attention to private feedback provided by guests. Even if it's not publicly visible, addressing concerns raised in private feedback contributes to overall guest satisfaction and may prevent negative public reviews.

9. Encourage Honest Reviews:

Encourage guests to leave honest reviews. Genuine feedback, both positive and negative, provides valuable insights and contributes to the authenticity of your hosting profile. An honest review culture fosters trust within the Airbnb community.

10. Keep a Positive Tone:

Maintain a positive and professional tone in your responses, even when addressing negative feedback. Avoid becoming defensive and instead focus on finding solutions. A positive and solution-oriented approach reflects well on your hosting style.

11. Use Feedback to Enhance Guest Experience:

Use guest feedback as a tool for continuous improvement. Analyze patterns in reviews to identify recurring themes or areas for enhancement. Your commitment to refining the guest experience based on feedback contributes to long-term hosting success.

12. Manage Unfair or Inaccurate Reviews:

If faced with unfair or inaccurate reviews, respond diplomatically and address the concerns professionally. Provide context or clarifications but avoid engaging in confrontations. Presenting your perspective in a calm and composed manner can mitigate the impact of unjust reviews.

13. Monitor Trends and Patterns:

Monitor trends and patterns in your reviews over time. Identify aspects that consistently receive praise and areas that may require attention. This ongoing analysis helps you adapt and refine your hosting approach to align with guest expectations.

14. Celebrate Positive Feedback:

Celebrate positive feedback with your hosting team or support network. Acknowledging and appreciating positive reviews is not just personally rewarding but also reinforces a positive hosting environment.

Mastering the art of handling guest reviews and feedback is an integral part of becoming a successful Airbnb host. By leveraging feedback as a tool for growth, responding thoughtfully, and continuously refining your hosting approach, you contribute to a positive guest experience and build a reputation that resonates within the Airbnb community.

Chapter 9 ~ Scaling Your Airbnb Business

Expanding to Multiple Properties

Expanding your Airbnb hosting venture to manage multiple properties is a significant step that comes with unique challenges and opportunities. This chapter explores the considerations and strategies for successfully scaling your hosting business:

1. Establish a Solid Foundation:

> Before expanding, ensure that your current Airbnb property is running smoothly and efficiently. Establishing a solid foundation ensures that you have the experience and systems in place to manage multiple properties effectively.

2. Develop Standard Operating Procedures (SOPs):

> Create comprehensive standard operating procedures (SOPs) for your hosting activities. SOPs provide a structured framework for managing each property, ensuring consistency in guest experiences and streamlining your management approach.

3. Delegate Responsibilities:

Recognize the importance of delegation as you expand. Whether hiring a property manager or collaborating with a trusted team, distributing responsibilities helps manage the increased workload and allows you to focus on strategic aspects of your hosting business.

4. Leverage Technology:

Embrace technology to streamline operations. Utilize property management software to handle bookings, automate communications, and track maintenance tasks across multiple properties. Technology enhances efficiency and reduces the administrative burden of managing a growing portfolio.

5. Understand Local Regulations:

Familiarize yourself with local regulations and zoning laws for each property. Regulations can vary significantly, and compliance is crucial to avoid legal issues. Understanding the legal landscape ensures that each property operates within the confines of local laws.

6. Cultivate a Reliable Support Network:

Cultivate a reliable support network of contractors, cleaners, and maintenance professionals. Having a trusted team in place is essential for addressing property-specific needs promptly and maintaining a high standard of quality across all your listings.

7. Diversify Property Locations:

Consider diversifying the locations of your properties. Having listings in different neighborhoods or cities can reduce the risk associated with local market fluctuations and broaden your potential guest base.

8. Develop a Brand Identity:

Create a brand identity for your Airbnb business. This includes consistent branding across listings, a unified theme in property decor, and a cohesive online presence. A strong brand identity contributes to guest trust and loyalty.

9. Monitor Market Trends:

Stay informed about market trends and demand in different locations. Regularly assess the performance of each property and adjust your strategy based on market dynamics. Flexibility and adaptability are key to success in a dynamic hospitality landscape.

10. Financial Planning and Budgeting:

Develop a comprehensive financial plan and budget for each property. Factor in operating costs, property management fees, marketing expenses, and any potential renovations or improvements. A robust financial strategy is essential for sustainable growth.

11. Implement Cross-Promotion Strategies:

Implement cross-promotion strategies across your properties. Encourage guests from one property to explore your other listings, offering incentives such as discounts for repeat bookings. Cross-promotion maximizes the visibility of your entire portfolio.

12. Stay Hands-On and Accessible:

While expanding, remain hands-on and accessible to both guests and your property management team. Maintain open communication channels, address guest inquiries promptly, and ensure that each property receives the attention it deserves.

13. Periodic Property Assessments:

Conduct periodic assessments of each property to identify areas for improvement. This could involve updates to decor, renovations, or technology upgrades. Regular assessments contribute to the long-term success and competitiveness of your listings.

14. Embrace Continuous Learning:

Approach the expansion process with a mindset of continuous learning. Each property and location presents unique challenges and opportunities. Embracing a learning-oriented approach allows you to refine your strategy and adapt to evolving market trends.

Expanding to multiple properties requires a strategic approach, meticulous planning, and a commitment to maintaining high standards across your entire portfolio. By incorporating these considerations into your expansion strategy, you position yourself for success in managing a thriving and diverse Airbnb hosting business.

Chapter: Hiring Staff or Outsourcing Tasks

As your Airbnb hosting venture grows, the demands on your time and resources increase. Deciding whether to hire staff or outsource tasks is a crucial step in optimizing your efficiency and ensuring the continued success of your hosting business. This chapter explores the considerations and strategies for making informed decisions in this aspect of your hosting journey:

1. Assess Your Workload:

> Begin by assessing your current workload and the tasks that consume most of your time. Identify areas where additional support or expertise could enhance efficiency and allow you to focus on strategic aspects of your hosting business.

2. Define Roles and Responsibilities:

> Clearly define roles and responsibilities for any staff or contractors you plan to hire. Establishing specific job descriptions helps set expectations and ensures that each team member understands their contributions to the overall success of the hosting venture.

3. Consider Property Management Companies:

Explore the option of partnering with property management companies. These professionals specialize in managing short-term rental properties and can handle various tasks, including guest communication, cleaning, and maintenance. Hiring a property management company can provide a comprehensive solution.

4. Identify Core Competencies:

Identify your core competencies and areas where your skills are most valuable. Tasks that fall outside your expertise or those that are time-consuming but do not directly contribute to guest satisfaction may be prime candidates for outsourcing or delegation.

5. Budget for Staff or Contractors:

Develop a budget for hiring staff or contractors. Consider factors such as salaries, benefits, or fees for outsourcing services. A well-structured budget ensures that the costs associated with additional support align with the financial health of your hosting business.

6. Determine Full-Time or Part-Time Needs:

Assess whether your hosting business requires full-time or part-time support. Depending on the scale of your operation, you may need dedicated staff or contractors for specific roles, or you may opt for part-time assistance to address seasonal demands.

7. Leverage Virtual Assistants:

Explore the benefits of hiring virtual assistants for tasks that can be performed remotely. Virtual assistants can handle administrative responsibilities, guest communications, and other non-location-specific tasks, offering flexibility and cost-effectiveness.

8. Retain Control Over Core Functions:

Retain control over core functions that require your personal touch or expertise. While outsourcing certain tasks can enhance efficiency, maintaining direct involvement in critical areas such as guest communication, property branding, and strategic decision-making is essential.

9. Vet and Train Your Team:

Whether hiring staff or outsourcing tasks, invest time in vetting and training your team. Ensure that they align with your hosting philosophy and understand the unique aspects of your properties. Effective training contributes to consistent service quality.

10. Establish Communication Protocols:

Establish clear communication protocols with your team. Define channels for regular updates, feedback, and emergency situations. Efficient communication is vital for maintaining a cohesive and well-coordinated hosting operation.

11. Monitor Performance Metrics:

Implement performance metrics to monitor the effectiveness of your staff or contractors. Track key performance indicators (KPIs) related to guest satisfaction, property maintenance, and other relevant areas. Regular assessments allow you to refine your team management strategies.

12. Adapt to Seasonal Demands:

Consider the seasonal demands of your hosting business when making staffing decisions. You may need additional support during peak seasons and can adjust staffing levels accordingly to ensure a smooth operation.

13. Explore Collaborative Platforms:

Explore collaborative platforms that connect hosts with freelance professionals. These platforms offer a pool of skilled individuals who can assist with tasks ranging from photography and content creation to property management and guest communication.

14. Embrace Flexibility and Adaptability:

Embrace flexibility and adaptability in your staffing approach. The needs of your hosting business may evolve, and having a flexible staffing strategy allows you to adjust to changing circumstances while maintaining operational efficiency.

Making informed decisions about hiring staff or outsourcing tasks is a critical aspect of scaling your Airbnb hosting venture. By carefully assessing your needs, defining roles, and implementing effective management strategies, you position yourself to optimize your time and resources while providing an exceptional experience for your guests.

Diversifying Your Offerings (e.g., Experiences, Guided Tours)

Expanding beyond traditional accommodation offerings can not only enhance your Airbnb hosting business but also provide unique and memorable experiences for your guests. This chapter explores the strategies and considerations for diversifying your offerings, including experiences, guided tours, and other supplementary services:

1. Explore Airbnb Experiences:

> Consider becoming an Airbnb Experience host. Airbnb Experiences allow you to offer unique activities, workshops, or tours that showcase your local expertise and passion. This adds an extra dimension to your hosting business and attracts guests seeking immersive and authentic experiences.

2. Identify Your Expertise and Interests:

> Identify your personal expertise and interests when developing experiences or guided tours. Leverage

your knowledge of the local area, cultural insights, or specific skills to create offerings that resonate with guests and showcase the uniqueness of your hosting location.

3. Tailor Experiences to Your Location:

Tailor experiences to the unique features of your location. Whether it's a culinary tour, outdoor adventure, or cultural exploration, align your offerings with the attractions and activities that make your hosting area special.

4. Collaborate with Local Businesses:

Collaborate with local businesses to enhance your offerings. Partnering with local guides, chefs, or artists can elevate the quality of your experiences and provide guests with a well-rounded and curated perspective of the destination.

5. Offer Customizable Packages:

Provide customizable packages that cater to different guest preferences. Some guests may be interested in a full-day guided tour, while others may prefer shorter, hands-on workshops. Offering a range of options increases the appeal of your experiences.

6. Highlight Sustainability and Responsible Tourism:

Integrate sustainability and responsible tourism practices into your offerings. Consider eco-friendly experiences, support local artisans and businesses, and emphasize the importance of responsible travel. This appeals to a growing segment of conscious travelers.

7. Incorporate Guest Feedback:

Incorporate guest feedback into the development and refinement of your experiences. Listen to their suggestions and adapt your offerings based on their preferences. Guest input is valuable in ensuring that your experiences align with market demands.

8. Showcase Experiences in Your Listing:

Showcase your experiences prominently in your Airbnb listing. Clearly communicate the unique activities or tours you offer, complete with engaging descriptions and high-quality visuals. This attracts guests who are specifically looking for immersive experiences in addition to accommodation.

9. Leverage Social Media for Promotion:

Utilize social media platforms to promote your experiences. Share captivating content, behind-the-scenes glimpses, and guest testimonials to create buzz around your offerings. Social media is a powerful tool for reaching a broader audience and building anticipation for your experiences.

10. Develop Packages for Special Occasions:

Create packages tailored for special occasions such as birthdays, anniversaries, or celebrations. Offering themed experiences adds a personalized touch and attracts guests looking for unique ways to commemorate significant moments during their travels.

11. Provide Seamless Booking Integration:

Ensure seamless integration for guests to book experiences directly through your Airbnb listing. Streamlining the booking process makes it convenient for guests to add curated experiences to their stay, enhancing the overall appeal of your hosting business.

12. Stay Informed about Local Events:

Stay informed about local events and festivals. Incorporating these events into your offerings allows you to capitalize on increased tourist activity and provides guests with opportunities to participate in community celebrations.

13. Offer Virtual Experiences:

Consider offering virtual experiences for guests who may prefer remote or online activities. Virtual experiences open up your offerings to a global audience and provide flexibility for guests with diverse interests.

14. Collaborate with Other Hosts:

Collaborate with fellow Airbnb hosts to create comprehensive experience packages. This collaborative approach allows you to combine strengths, offer diverse perspectives, and create multi-faceted experiences that cater to a broader range of interests.

Diversifying your offerings beyond traditional accommodations can significantly enhance the appeal of your Airbnb hosting business. By leveraging your local expertise, collaborating with partners, and providing unique and memorable experiences, you not only differentiate yourself in the market but also create lasting impressions for your guests.

Chapter 10 ~ Staying Legal and Compliant

Understanding Local Regulations and Zoning Laws

Navigating local regulations and zoning laws is a crucial aspect of establishing and maintaining a successful Airbnb hosting venture. This chapter provides insights and strategies for understanding and complying with the legal landscape governing short-term rentals in your area:

1. Research Local Regulations:

> Begin by thoroughly researching local regulations and zoning laws related to short-term rentals in your area. Regulations can vary widely, and understanding the specific rules that apply to your property is fundamental to compliance.

2. Consult with Local Authorities:

> Reach out to local authorities, such as municipal planning departments or zoning offices, for guidance. Seeking clarification directly from relevant authorities can provide accurate and up-to-date information on the regulations that pertain to your specific location.

3. Identify Permitting Requirements:

Determine whether permits or licenses are required for operating a short-term rental in your area. Some municipalities may mandate specific permits, and obtaining these authorizations is a critical step in legal compliance.

4. Know Occupancy Limits:

Familiarize yourself with occupancy limits set by local regulations. Understanding the maximum number of guests allowed can prevent violations and ensure that your property operates within legal parameters.

5. Be Aware of Tax Obligations:

Understand the tax obligations associated with short-term rentals in your jurisdiction. This may include occupancy taxes, sales taxes, or other local levies. Complying with tax regulations is essential for avoiding legal complications.

6. Respect Zoning Designations:

Respect zoning designations for your property. Zoning laws dictate how properties can be used in specific areas, and short-term rentals may be subject to zoning restrictions. Ensure that your property aligns with its designated use within the local zoning plan.

7. Stay Informed about Changes:

Stay informed about any changes to local regulations. The legal landscape for short-term rentals can evolve, and being aware of updates or amendments ensures that you adapt your hosting practices to remain in compliance.

8. Establish Open Communication:

Establish open communication with your neighbors. Inform them about your intention to operate a short-term rental and address any concerns they may have. Building positive relationships with neighbors can contribute to a harmonious hosting environment.

9. Be Mindful of Homeowners Associations (HOAs):

If your property is part of a homeowner's association (HOA), be mindful of any additional rules or restrictions they may have regarding short-term rentals. HOA regulations can complement or differ from local laws, and compliance is essential on both fronts.

10. Seek Legal Advice if Necessary:

If navigating local regulations becomes complex, consider seeking legal advice. Consulting with an attorney experienced in real estate and hospitality law can provide tailored guidance and help you navigate potential legal challenges.

11. Implement Safety Measures:

Prioritize safety measures in accordance with local regulations. This may include installing safety equipment, adhering to fire codes, or implementing emergency procedures. Ensuring the safety of your guests and property is a fundamental aspect of legal compliance.

12. Monitor Noise Regulations:

Be aware of noise regulations in your area. Many municipalities have specific rules regarding noise levels, especially during certain hours. Establishing clear guidelines for guests and monitoring noise levels helps prevent legal issues related to noise complaints.

13. Keep Detailed Records:

Keep detailed records of permits, licenses, and any communications with local authorities. Maintaining comprehensive documentation demonstrates your commitment to compliance and serves as evidence in case of legal inquiries.

14. Join Local Hosting Associations:

Consider joining local hosting associations or networks. These groups often provide valuable insights into local regulations, offer support from experienced hosts, and advocate for the interests of short-term rental operators within the community.

Understanding and adhering to local regulations and zoning laws are essential components of responsible and sustainable Airbnb hosting. By proactively engaging with the legal landscape, staying informed, and seeking support when needed, you position yourself to operate within the parameters of the law while providing a positive and compliant hosting experience.

Obtaining Necessary Permits and Licenses

Securing the required permits and licenses is a critical step in establishing a legal and compliant Airbnb hosting business. This chapter outlines the key considerations and steps to obtain the necessary authorizations for your short-term rental:

1. Research Local Permitting Requirements:

Begin by researching local permitting requirements for short-term rentals in your area. Understand the specific permits and licenses needed to legally operate your Airbnb business. This information is often available through municipal websites or local government offices.

2. Contact Local Authorities:

Reach out to local authorities, such as the planning department or zoning office, to confirm the necessary permits for your property. Direct communication ensures you receive accurate and up-to-date information tailored to your specific location.

3. Identify and Understand Permit Types:

Identify the types of permits required for your short-term rental. Common permits may include a short-term rental permit, business license, or health and safety permits. Understand the purpose and conditions associated with each type of permit.

4. Determine Eligibility Criteria:

Determine the eligibility criteria for obtaining permits. Some permits may have specific requirements related to property size, zoning designations, or safety standards. Ensure that your property meets the criteria outlined for each permit.

5. Gather Necessary Documentation:

Gather the necessary documentation required for permit applications. This may include property ownership records, floor plans, safety certificates, and any other documentation specified by local authorities. Having a complete set of documents streamlines the application process.

6. Attend Permitting Workshops or Meetings:

Attend permitting workshops or meetings hosted by local authorities. These sessions often provide valuable information about the application process, eligibility criteria, and any recent updates to local regulations. Attendees can ask questions and seek clarification on specific concerns.

7. Complete Permit Applications:

Complete permit applications accurately and thoroughly. Pay close attention to details, provide all required information, and ensure that your application adheres to local guidelines. Incomplete or inaccurate applications can lead to delays in the permitting process.

8. Pay Application Fees:

Be prepared to pay application fees associated with obtaining permits. These fees may cover the administrative costs of processing applications. Familiarize yourself with the fee structure and submit payments in a timely manner.

9. Adhere to Timelines:

Adhere to application timelines specified by local authorities. Some permits may have expiration dates, and compliance with application deadlines is crucial for obtaining and maintaining the necessary authorizations for your short-term rental.

10. Address Conditions or Modifications:

Be open to addressing any conditions or modifications requested by local authorities during the permitting process. Authorities may provide feedback or request adjustments to ensure compliance with regulations. Respond promptly and collaborate to resolve any concerns.

11. Display Permits as Required:

Once permits are obtained, display them as required by local regulations. This may involve visibly posting permits within your property or providing permit information in your Airbnb listing. Compliance with display requirements is essential for transparency and legal adherence.

12. Renew Permits as Necessary:

Be aware of permit renewal requirements. Some permits may need to be renewed annually, and staying current with renewals is essential for continuous legal operation. Set reminders well in advance of expiration dates to ensure timely renewal.

13. Stay Informed about Changes:

Stay informed about changes to permitting requirements. Local regulations may evolve, and staying updated on any amendments or new regulations ensures that your short-term rental remains in compliance with current laws.

14. Seek Professional Guidance if Needed:

If the permitting process seems complex, consider seeking professional guidance. Engage with legal professionals or consultants experienced in short-term rental regulations. Their expertise can provide valuable insights and ensure a smooth permitting process.

Obtaining the necessary permits and licenses is a foundational step in building a legal and successful Airbnb hosting business. By proactively engaging with local authorities, adhering to regulations, and staying informed about changes, you establish a framework for responsible and compliant hosting.

Staying Updated on Changes in Airbnb Policies

Remaining informed about changes in Airbnb policies is crucial for maintaining a successful and compliant hosting business. This chapter outlines strategies to stay abreast of policy updates and navigate the evolving landscape of Airbnb's guidelines:

1. Regularly Review Airbnb's Official Resources:

> Make it a habit to regularly review Airbnb's official resources, including the Airbnb website, host newsletters, and policy documentation. Airbnb communicates important updates and changes through these channels, providing hosts with the latest information.

2. Subscribe to Host Newsletters:

> Subscribe to Airbnb's host newsletters and updates. These newsletters often contain policy changes, feature announcements, and tips for hosts. By subscribing, you ensure that relevant information is delivered directly to your inbox.

3. Join Host Forums and Communities:

Participate in host forums and communities where hosts share information and experiences. Platforms like the Airbnb Community Center or independent host groups on social media provide spaces for hosts to discuss policy changes and share insights. Engaging in these communities can offer valuable perspectives.

4. Attend Airbnb Webinars and Events:

Attend webinars or events hosted by Airbnb. These sessions may cover policy updates, best practices, and upcoming features. Participating in live events allows you to ask questions and gain clarity on any uncertainties related to policy changes.

5. Monitor Host Dashboards and Notifications:

Regularly check your host dashboard for notifications and updates from Airbnb. The dashboard often displays important messages regarding policy changes, upcoming requirements, or announcements that directly impact hosts.

6. Follow Airbnb on Social Media:

Follow Airbnb's official social media accounts. Platforms like Twitter, Facebook, and Instagram may feature announcements and updates related to policies and features. Social media can serve as a quick and accessible source of information.

7. Engage with Airbnb Support:

Reach out to Airbnb Support for clarification on specific policies or changes. If you have questions or uncertainties, contacting Airbnb directly can provide you with official guidance and ensure that you have accurate information.

8. Review Terms of Service and Community Standards:

Regularly review Airbnb's Terms of Service and Community Standards. These documents outline the rules and expectations for hosts and guests. Understanding the terms and standards helps you align your hosting practices with Airbnb's guidelines.

9. Attend Host Education Programs:

Take advantage of host education programs offered by Airbnb. These programs may cover a range of topics, including policy updates, responsible hosting practices, and guest communication strategies. Education programs enhance your understanding of Airbnb's evolving landscape.

10. Set Notifications for Policy Changes:

Enable notifications for policy changes on your Airbnb account settings. By opting to receive notifications, you ensure that you are promptly alerted to any updates or modifications in Airbnb's policies that may impact your hosting practices.

11. Collaborate with Local Airbnb Representatives:

If available, collaborate with local Airbnb representatives. They may host informational sessions or provide insights into region-specific policy changes. Establishing a connection with local representatives enhances your understanding of policies applicable to your hosting location.

12. Network with Experienced Hosts:

Network with experienced hosts who are well-versed in Airbnb policies. Experienced hosts can share practical insights and tips for navigating policy changes based on their own experiences. Learning from their expertise can be invaluable.

13. Be Proactive in Seeking Information:

Be proactive in seeking information about policy changes. Don't wait for issues to arise; actively seek updates and clarifications to ensure that you are well-prepared and compliant with the latest Airbnb guidelines.

14. Adapt and Implement Changes Promptly:

Once aware of policy changes, adapt and implement them promptly. Being proactive in aligning your hosting practices with updated policies not only ensures compliance but also contributes to a positive hosting experience for both you and your guests.

Staying updated on changes in Airbnb policies is a proactive and essential aspect of successful hosting. By utilizing official resources, engaging with the Airbnb community, and maintaining open communication with the platform, you position yourself as an informed and responsible host in the ever-evolving landscape of short-term rentals.

Conclusion

Part 1: Reflecting on the Journey as an Airbnb Entrepreneur

As you reach the culmination of this guide on becoming an Airbnb host, it's a fitting moment to pause and reflect on the transformative journey you've undertaken. Becoming an Airbnb entrepreneur is not merely a venture into short-term rental hosting; it's an exploration of hospitality, business acumen, and the art of creating memorable experiences for guests. Let's delve into some key reflections on your journey:

1. Embracing Entrepreneurial Spirit:

> Throughout this guide, you've embraced the entrepreneurial spirit that defines successful Airbnb hosts. You've navigated the intricacies of the platform, harnessed your creativity, and cultivated a business mindset to establish and grow your hosting venture.

2. Navigating Challenges and Learning Opportunities:

> Every step in your Airbnb journey has presented its unique set of challenges and learning opportunities. Whether it was understanding local regulations,

refining your hosting strategy, or adapting to policy changes, each challenge has contributed to your growth as an informed and resilient host.

3. Crafting a Unique Hosting Identity:

Your hosting venture is a reflection of your unique identity and vision. From crafting appealing property descriptions to offering personalized experiences, you've infused your hosting style with authenticity. This individuality not only sets you apart in a competitive market but also forms the core of memorable guest experiences.

4. Balancing Innovation and Adaptability:

Successful Airbnb entrepreneurship thrives on a delicate balance between innovation and adaptability. You've embraced new features, explored diverse offerings, and remained flexible in response to market dynamics. This adaptive approach positions you to thrive in an ever-evolving landscape.

5. Cultivating a Guest-Centric Approach:

At the heart of your journey is a guest-centric approach. You've prioritized guest satisfaction, crafted welcoming spaces, and gone above and beyond to create a hospitable environment. This commitment to guest experience is the foundation of positive reviews and sustained success.

6. Nurturing Collaborative Connections:

Becoming an Airbnb entrepreneur isn't just about managing properties; it's about building connections. Whether collaborating with local businesses, networking with fellow hosts, or engaging with Airbnb support, you've recognized the value of collaborative relationships in fostering a thriving hosting community.

7. Embracing Continuous Learning:

Your journey as an Airbnb host is an ongoing process of learning and growth. You've embraced new information, sought insights from experienced hosts, and demonstrated a willingness to adapt based on evolving market trends and platform dynamics. This commitment to continuous learning positions you as a dynamic and informed host.

8. Upholding Ethical and Legal Standards:

The ethical and legal considerations of hosting have been central to your journey. From understanding local regulations to obtaining necessary permits, you've upheld the standards of responsible hosting. Operating within legal parameters not only safeguards your business but also contributes to the integrity of the broader hosting community.

9. Celebrating Successes, Big and Small:

Take a moment to celebrate your successes, both big and small. Whether it's achieving Superhost status, receiving positive guest reviews, or successfully expanding your hosting portfolio, each milestone is a testament to your dedication and the positive impact you've made on the Airbnb platform.

As you reflect on the insights gained and the strategies implemented throughout this guide, you're equipped with a comprehensive understanding of the Airbnb hosting landscape. The journey doesn't end here; it evolves into a continual cycle of refinement, innovation, and a commitment to providing exceptional experiences for your guests. In the next section of the conclusion, we'll delve into strategic considerations for the future and outline actionable steps to propel your Airbnb entrepreneurship to new heights.

Part 2: Encouraging Others to Explore the Possibilities of Airbnb Hosting

As you reflect on your own transformative journey as an Airbnb host, it's an opportune moment to extend an invitation to others who may be considering embarking on this rewarding venture. Airbnb hosting is not just about managing properties; it's about crafting unique experiences, building connections, and embracing the entrepreneurial spirit. In this section, we explore the possibilities of Airbnb hosting and encourage others to embark on their own exciting journey:

1. Embracing the Spirit of Hospitality:

> Airbnb hosting invites individuals to embrace the spirit of hospitality in a way that goes beyond traditional accommodations. Whether you have a spare room, an entire property, or an idea for a unique experience, hosting provides a platform to share your

passion, culture, and local insights with guests from around the world.

2. Unlocking Creativity in Hosting Spaces:

The canvas of Airbnb hosting allows for boundless creativity in designing and presenting spaces. From cozy apartments to eclectic homes, hosts have the opportunity to showcase their unique style and create an immersive environment that resonates with guests.

3. Cultivating Meaningful Connections:

Hosting on Airbnb is not just about providing a place to stay; it's about cultivating meaningful connections. As a host, you have the chance to interact with guests, share stories, and create memorable experiences that go beyond the transactional nature of traditional accommodations.

4. Flexibility in Hosting Approaches:

Airbnb accommodates various hosting approaches, making it accessible to a diverse range of individuals. Whether you're interested in renting out a spare room, managing multiple properties, or offering specialized experiences, the flexibility of the platform allows hosts to tailor their approach to their preferences and goals.

5. Supporting Local Economies:

Airbnb hosting contributes to supporting local economies. By recommending nearby businesses, collaborating with local artisans, and introducing guests to hidden gems in the community, hosts play a vital role in promoting economic growth and sustainability.

6. Entrepreneurial Opportunities:

For those with an entrepreneurial spirit, Airbnb hosting presents a canvas for innovative ideas and business ventures. Whether it's creating unique experiences, collaborating with local businesses, or expanding to manage multiple properties, the entrepreneurial possibilities within the Airbnb ecosystem are vast.

7. Fostering a Global Community:

Airbnb fosters a global community of hosts and travelers. By opening your doors to guests from different corners of the world, you become part of a network that celebrates diversity, cultural exchange, and the shared joy of exploration.

8. Positive Impact on Travel Culture:

Hosting on Airbnb contributes to shaping a positive travel culture. Through responsible hosting practices, hosts can influence a shift towards sustainable and community-driven tourism, creating a more enriching travel experience for guests and locals alike.

9. Empowering Others to Explore Hosting:

As a seasoned Airbnb host, you have the opportunity to empower others to explore the possibilities of hosting. Share your insights, offer guidance, and encourage those intrigued by the idea of hosting to take the first step. Your experience can serve as inspiration for others to embark on their own hosting adventure.

10. Inviting Future Innovations:

The landscape of Airbnb hosting is dynamic, with the potential for future innovations and exciting possibilities. By encouraging others to join the hosting community, you contribute to the ongoing evolution of Airbnb, shaping the future of travel and hospitality.

11. Celebrating the Diversity of Hosting Stories:

Every Airbnb host has a unique story to tell. Celebrate the diversity of hosting stories and encourage others to add their own chapters. Whether it's through homestays, boutique experiences, or innovative hosting models, each story contributes to the rich tapestry of the Airbnb hosting community.

In concluding this guide, consider extending an invitation to those who may be contemplating the journey of Airbnb hosting. By sharing the possibilities, encouraging creativity, and fostering a spirit of community, you contribute to the vibrant and ever-expanding world of Airbnb hosting. May your hosting journey continue to be filled with exploration, connection, and the fulfillment of both personal and entrepreneurial aspirations.

Part 3: Final Tips for Success and Sustainability

As you approach the final section of this guide, consider it a roadmap for sustained success and meaningful impact as an Airbnb host. These concluding tips encapsulate key principles to guide you towards long-term prosperity in your hosting journey:

1. Prioritize Guest Experience:

The cornerstone of successful Airbnb hosting lies in prioritizing the guest experience. Strive to create welcoming, comfortable, and memorable spaces that resonate with your guests. Anticipate their needs, offer thoughtful amenities, and go the extra mile to ensure their stay is exceptional.

2. Maintain Clear Communication:

Effective communication is key to a positive hosting experience. Be transparent in your listing descriptions, respond promptly to guest inquiries, and communicate clearly throughout the booking process. Establishing open lines of communication fosters trust and sets the foundation for a smooth guest-host relationship.

3. Embrace Continuous Improvement:

Commit to a mindset of continuous improvement. Regularly evaluate your hosting practices, seek feedback from guests, and adapt based on evolving market trends. Embracing a culture of continuous improvement positions you as a dynamic host in a competitive landscape.

4. Leverage Technology Wisely:

Embrace technology to streamline your hosting operations. Utilize Airbnb's host tools, leverage smart home devices for efficiency, and explore innovative solutions to enhance the guest experience. Technology can be a powerful ally in managing your properties and staying ahead in the competitive hosting arena.

5. Foster Positive Reviews and Ratings:

Positive reviews and high ratings are invaluable assets in the world of Airbnb. Prioritize guest satisfaction, address concerns promptly, and exceed expectations to garner positive feedback. Positive reviews not only attract more guests but also contribute to your Superhost status.

6. Stay Informed about Market Trends:

Stay informed about market trends and industry developments. Regularly monitor Airbnb's updates, engage with host communities, and be aware of broader trends in the travel and hospitality sector.

Adapting to changing market dynamics positions you as a savvy and informed host.

7. Practice Responsible Hosting:

Responsible hosting is not only ethically sound but also crucial for long-term sustainability. Adhere to local regulations, obtain necessary permits, and implement eco-friendly practices where possible. Responsible hosting contributes to the positive image of the Airbnb community.

8. Diversify Offerings for Sustainability:

Explore opportunities to diversify your offerings. Consider expanding to different types of properties, offering unique experiences, or collaborating with local businesses. Diversification not only enhances your revenue streams but also insulates your business against market fluctuations.

9. Nurture Community Connections:

Cultivate connections within the hosting community and the local neighborhood. Collaborate with fellow hosts, share insights, and engage with local businesses. Building a strong network contributes to a sense of community and provides valuable support in your hosting journey.

10. Plan for Maintenance and Upkeep:

Plan for the maintenance and upkeep of your properties. Set aside funds for routine maintenance, repairs, and occasional upgrades. A well-maintained property not only attracts positive reviews but also ensures the long-term sustainability of your hosting business.

11. Balance Occupancy with Rest:

Strive for a healthy balance between high occupancy rates and personal well-being. Avoid burnout by scheduling breaks between bookings, setting realistic availability, and establishing a support system to manage your hosting responsibilities. A rested host is better equipped to provide a quality guest experience.

12. Monitor Financial Performance:

Keep a close eye on the financial performance of your hosting business. Regularly assess income and expenses, track financial goals, and adjust your strategy as needed. Monitoring financial performance is essential for the sustained success and growth of your hosting venture.

13. Embrace Sustainability Practices:

Consider implementing sustainability practices in your hosting operations. From energy-efficient appliances to waste reduction initiatives, incorporating sustainable practices not only aligns with growing environmental consciousness but also appeals to an increasing number of eco-conscious travelers.

14. Celebrate Milestones and Achievements:

Take the time to celebrate milestones and achievements in your hosting journey. Whether it's achieving Superhost status, expanding your portfolio, or receiving a particularly positive review, recognizing and celebrating your successes reinforces your commitment to excellence.

As you integrate these final tips into your hosting strategy, remember that the journey as an Airbnb host is a dynamic and evolving one. By embracing the principles of excellence, sustainability, and continuous improvement, you position yourself for enduring success and a positive impact within the vibrant community of Airbnb hosts. May your hosting venture continue to thrive and bring fulfillment, both personally and professionally.

Appendix

Recommended Tools for Managing Airbnb Listings

Efficiently managing your Airbnb listings requires a strategic combination of organization, communication, and automation. The following tools are recommended to streamline various aspects of your hosting operations, enhance guest experiences, and contribute to the overall success of your Airbnb venture:

1. Airbnb Host Dashboard:

Purpose: Centralized platform provided by Airbnb for managing your listings, guest communications, and reservations.

Key Features:

- Calendar management

- Message center for guest communication

- Reservation details and payment tracking

2. Smartbnb:

Purpose: Automate guest communication and enhance the guest experience.

Key Features:

  - Automated messaging for check-in instructions and other information

  - Multi-language support

  - Integration with Airbnb for seamless communication

3. Guesty:

Purpose: Comprehensive property management platform for Airbnb hosts managing multiple listings.

Key Features:

  - Channel management for multiple platforms

  - Reservation system and payment processing

  - Task automation for cleaning and maintenance

4. PriceLabs:

Purpose: Dynamic pricing tool for optimizing rental rates based on market demand and other factors.

Key Features:

- Automated pricing adjustments

- Customizable pricing rules

- Integration with various property management systems

5. KeyNest:

Purpose: Key exchange solution for secure and convenient guest check-ins.

Key Features:

- Secure key storage at local businesses

- Contactless check-ins for guests

- Real-time monitoring of key usage

6. NoiseAware:

Purpose: Monitor and address noise levels in your property to ensure compliance with local regulations.

Key Features:

- Noise monitoring sensors

- Real-time alerts for excessive noise

- Historical noise level reports

7. Beyond Pricing:

Purpose: Automated pricing tool with a focus on maximizing revenue for hosts.

Key Features:

- Dynamic pricing adjustments based on market trends

- Integration with various property management systems

- Competitor analysis for pricing optimization

8. YourWelcome:

Purpose: Digital welcome book and guest communication tool.

Key Features:

- Digital welcome book with local recommendations

- In-app messaging for guest communication

- Check-out instructions and feedback collection

9. Properly:

Purpose: Task management and cleaning coordination for hosts with multiple listings.

Key Features:

- Cleaning checklists and visual guides

- Task assignment and tracking

- Integration with various property management systems

10. Hostfully:

Purpose: Create and share digital guidebooks for guests with local recommendations.

Key Features:

- Customizable guidebooks with property details

- Integration with Airbnb for automatic syncing

- Guest communication features

11. Tokeet:

Purpose: Comprehensive property management and booking platform.

Key Features:

- Reservation system and payment processing

- Channel management for multiple platforms

- Task automation for cleaning and maintenance

12. Smart Locks (e.g., August, Schlage Encode):

Purpose: Keyless entry solutions for secure and convenient guest access.

Key Features:

- Remote access control

- Temporary access codes for guests

- Integration with smart home systems

These tools are designed to simplify various aspects of managing Airbnb listings, from communication and pricing optimization to key exchange and property maintenance. Depending on the scale and specific needs of your hosting business, consider integrating these tools to enhance efficiency, guest satisfaction, and overall success in your Airbnb venture.

Useful Websites for Staying Informed on Industry Trends

Staying informed about industry trends is crucial for the success and sustainability of your Airbnb hosting business. The following websites provide valuable insights, news, and updates on the evolving landscape of short-term rentals, travel, and hospitality:

1. Airbnb Community Center:

https://community.withairbnb.com/

Purpose: Connect with fellow hosts, share experiences, and stay updated on Airbnb announcements and community discussions.

2. Skift: https://skift.com/

Purpose: A leading platform covering global travel industry news, trends, and insights. Skift offers in-depth analysis and reports on the evolving dynamics of the travel and hospitality sector.

3. VRM Intel: https://www.vrmintel.com/

Purpose: Dedicated to vacation rental management, VRM Intel provides news, articles, and resources specifically tailored for property managers and vacation rental professionals.

4. AllTheRooms: https://www.alltherooms.com/

Purpose: A comprehensive platform offering insights into vacation rentals, hotels, and alternative accommodations. AllTheRooms provides data-driven analytics and trends in the hospitality industry.

5. The Airbnb Blog: https://www.airbnb.com/blog

Purpose: Airbnb's official blog shares updates, feature announcements, and stories from hosts and guests. It's a valuable resource for understanding platform changes and best practices.

6. AirDNA: https://www.airdna.co/

Purpose: AirDNA specializes in data and analytics for short-term rentals. Their blog and reports offer market insights, pricing trends, and performance analysis for Airbnb hosts.

7. Lodgify Blog: https://www.lodgify.com/blog/

Purpose: Lodgify's blog focuses on vacation rental management, providing tips, industry insights, and best practices for hosts looking to optimize their property management.

8. Hostfully Blog: https://www.hostfully.com/blog

Purpose: Hostfully's blog covers topics related to hospitality, guest experiences, and vacation rental management. It's a valuable resource for hosts seeking practical insights.

9. Booking.com Partner Hub: https://partner.booking.com/en-gb

Purpose: While primarily for partners of Booking.com, the Partner Hub often features articles and resources on industry trends and best practices in the broader accommodation sector.

10. PhocusWire: https://www.phocuswire.com/

Purpose: PhocusWire covers global travel technology news and trends. It's a valuable resource for hosts interested in the intersection of technology and the travel industry.

11. Tnooz: https://www.tnooz.com/

Purpose: Tnooz provides insights into travel technology, distribution, and digital marketing. It's a useful source for staying informed about the latest trends shaping the travel landscape.

12. HospitalityNet: https://www.hospitalitynet.org/

Purpose: Covering the global hospitality industry, HospitalityNet offers news, articles, and analysis on trends affecting hotels, vacation rentals, and accommodations.

As you navigate the dynamic world of Airbnb hosting, regularly visiting these websites will help you stay informed about industry trends, regulatory changes, and best practices. Incorporating these insights into your hosting strategy positions you as an informed and proactive participant in the evolving landscape of short-term rentals.

Templates for Communication with Guests, House Rules, and Guides

Effective communication with guests is a key aspect of successful Airbnb hosting. Below are templates you can use as a starting point for various communication needs, including welcoming messages, house rules, and local guides.

1. Welcome Message Template:

Subject: Welcome to [Your Property Name]!

Hi [Guest's Name],Welcome to [Your Property Name]! We're thrilled to have you as our guest. I hope you have a smooth journey and enjoy your stay with us.

Check-In Information:

- Check-in time: [Specify Check-in Time]

- Key or Access Code: [Provide Key or Access Code Details]

- Wi-Fi Network: [Wi-Fi Network Name]

- Password: [Wi-Fi Password]

If you have any questions or need assistance during your stay, feel free to reach out. We've included some local recommendations and important information about the property below.

Safe travels, and we look forward to hosting you!

2. House Rules Template:

Welcome to [Your Property Name]!

Dear Guests,

We're delighted to welcome you to our home. To ensure a pleasant stay for everyone, we kindly ask you to adhere to the following house rules:

1. Check-in/Check-out:

   - Check-in: [Specify Check-in Time]

   - Check-out: [Specify Check-out Time]

2. Quiet Hours:

   - Please observe quiet hours from [Start Time] to [End Time].

3. No Smoking:

Smoking is strictly prohibited inside the property. Designated outdoor smoking areas are provided.

4. Pets:

Unfortunately, we cannot accommodate pets.

5. Guest Limit:

The maximum number of guests allowed is [Specify Maximum Number].

6. Events and Parties:

Parties and events are not permitted on the premises.

7. Respect for Neighbors:

Please be considerate of our neighbors by keeping noise levels down.

8. Security and Access:

Ensure that all doors and windows are securely locked when leaving the property.

We appreciate your cooperation in maintaining a respectful and enjoyable environment. If you have any questions or concerns, feel free to reach out.

Thank you,

[Your Name]

3. Local Guide Template:

Discover [Your Location]: A Local Guide for Our Guests

Welcome to [Your Location]! To make your stay even more enjoyable, we've compiled a list of local recommendations and important information:

Dining:

1. [Restaurant Name] - Cuisine: [Type of Cuisine], Address: [Restaurant Address]

2. [Restaurant Name] - Cuisine: [Type of Cuisine], Address: [Restaurant Address]

3. [Restaurant Name] - Cuisine: [Type of Cuisine], Address: [Restaurant Address]

Sightseeing:

1. [Attraction Name] - Description: [Brief Description], Address: [Attraction Address]

2. [Attraction Name] - Description: [Brief Description], Address: [Attraction Address]

3. [Attraction Name] - Description: [Brief Description], Address: [Attraction Address]

Transportation:

- Nearest Public Transport: [Details]

- Local Taxi Service: [Phone Number]

- Parking Information: [Details]

Emergency Contacts:

- Local Emergency Services: [Emergency Phone Number]

- Hospital: [Hospital Name and Phone Number]

We hope you have a wonderful time exploring [Your Location]. If you need any further assistance, feel free to reach out.

Feel free to customize these templates based on your property's specific details and your hosting style. Effective communication enhances the guest experience and contributes to positive reviews and successful hosting.